Vegetable Science for Competitive Examinations

NIPA® GENX ELECTRONIC RESOURCES & SOLUTIONS P. LTD.
New Delhi-110 034

About the Authors

Prof. Baseerat Afroza is presently working as Head/Professor in the Division of Vegetable Science, Faculty of Horticulture, SKUAST-Kashmir. She has done B.Sc, M.Sc (Vegetable Science) and Ph.D Vegetable Science from the SKUAST-K. She has been a gold medalist twice in her B.Sc as well as in Doctorate degree programme. With a distinguished career spanning 23 years, Dr. Baseerat Afroza's contributions have significantly shaped the landscape of vegetable cultivation. As Head of the Division of Vegetable Science at SKUAST-K, her dedication to understanding, combating, and safeguarding is both unwavering and inspiring. The author is the member of many reputed societies and journals. She has to her credit more than 100 research publications, popular articles, manuals and technical bulletins. She is the recipient of various awards during conferences, workshops and seminars.

Dr. Syed Berjes Zehra is presently working as Assistant Professor in the Division of Vegetable Science, Faculty of Horticulture, SKUAST-Kashmir. She has done B.Sc Horticulture, M.Sc Horticulture (Vegetable Science) and Ph.D Vegetable Science from the SKUAST-K.She has been a gold medalist twice in her MSc as well as PhD programme. She has been Awarded with INSPIRE Fellowship by Ministry of Science and Technology Govt. Of India during Doctoral Programme. She has also qualified ASRB/ICAR NET. The author has a Research/Teaching/Extension experience besides working in an externally funded projects as a Co-PI including AICRP on vegetable crops. The author is guiding (as advisor & co-advisor) a number of students at UG and PG level. The author has a significant contribution of working in cold-arid region of Ladakh. The author has to her credit >20 Research papers besides a number of Review articles, Magazine articles, Abstracts in National and Internationalconferences,Book Chapters, Extension publications/ Manuals/Booklets. The author has coordinated a number of trainings/workshop besides she is a life member of society for community mobilization for sustainable development.

Dr. Asima Amin is presently working as Assistant Professor in Division of Vegetable Science, Faculty of Horticulture, SKUAST Kashmir, Shalimar 190025 (India). She has done her B.Sc. (Agriculture) from Sher-e-Kashmir University of Agricultural Science and Technology (SKUAST), Kashmir, J&K, M.Sc. Vegetable Science from Punjab Agricultural University, Ludhiana, Punjab and Ph.D from Sher-e-Kashmir University of Agricultural Science and Technology (SKUAST), Kashmir. During her Masters programme she was awarded Merit Fellowship and is Gold Medalist in Ph. D degree programme. She has done her Post Doctorate Fellowship from Indian Agricultural Research Institute (IARI), New Delhi. She has also qualified ASRB/ICAR NET. The author has Research/Teaching/Extension experience and has more than 40 research papers in national and international reputed journals with high impact factor. The author is guiding (as advisor & co-advisor) a number of students at UG and PG level. The author has to her credit a number of Review articles, Magazine articles, Abstracts in National and International conferences, Book Chapters, Extension publications/Manuals/Booklets. The author has coordinated a number of trainings/workshops. She has also to her credit 3 Edited book entitled "Unraveling Potato Viruses: Detection, Eradication and Crop Protection" published by Elite Publishing House, "Greenhouse Gardeners Companion" published by Elite Publishing House and "Seed production in Vegetable Crops" published by Elite Publishing House.

Dr. Gazala Nazir is presently working as Assistant Professor in the Division of Vegetable Science, Faculty of Horticulture, SKUAST-Kashmir. She has done BSc Horticulture, MSc Horticulture (Vegetable Science) and Ph.D Vegetable Science from the SKUAST-K. She has also qualified ASRB/ICAR NET. The author has nine years of experience in Extension and five years of teaching experience Besides working in some externally funded projects as a Co-PI.The author is guiding (as advisor & co-advisor) a number of students at UG and PG level.. The author has coordinated a number of trainings/ workshop besides she is a life member of society for community mobilization for sustainable development. The author has to her credit 27 Research papers, 6 Review articles, 6 Magazine articles, >30 Abstracts in National and International conferences, 4 Book Chapters, 11 Extension publications/Manuals/Booklets and 23 chapters in workshops/Summer schools/Seminar Proceedings, besides, she is a reviewer and life member of a number of national journals. She also has to her credit an Innovative article award (2022) for an article in Agriculture & Food: e-Newsletter. She has also organized almost 9 trainings and workshops as a co-ordinator

Dr. Ummyiah H. Masoodi is presently working as Assistant Professor in the Division of Vegetable Science, Faculty of Horticulture, SKUAST-Kashmir. She has done her BSc Agriculture, MSc Vegetable Science and PhD Vegetable Science from the same university and has been a gold medallist in her MSc as well as PhD. She has also qualified ASRB/ICAR NET. She has a teaching experience of more than 6 years at U.G. and P.G. level with a total of 87 credits for PG level courses and 71 credits for UG level courses so far. The author has supervised 16 UG students as advisor, 2 PhDs as a member of advisory committee, 8 MScs as member and 3 MScs as main advisor. The author has 11 yearsofresearch experience besides working in an externally funded project as a Co-PI. The author has to her credit 25 Research papers, 11 Review articles, 6 Magazine articles, >40 Abstracts in National and International conferences, 19 Book Chapters, 14 Extension publications/Manuals/Booklets and 25 chapters in workshops/Summer schools/Seminar proceedings, besides, she is a reviewer and life member of a number of national journals. She also has to her credit an Innovative article award (2022) for an article in Agriculture & Food: e-Newsletter. She has also organized almost 19 trainings and workshops as a co-ordinator. She has also to her credit 1 Edited book entitled"Vermicomposting-The Nature Friendly Technology" published by Elite Publishing House.

Prof. Shabir A Wani is presently working as Dean Faculty of Horticulture, SKUAST-Kashmir Srinagar. Dr. Wani has served in various capacities as scientist, senior scientist, Professor and Head in the in the division of Agricultural economics at SKUAST-K.During his 31 years of service, he has guided many students, authored 7 books in edited books, 8 policy papers, published more than 75 papers in peer reviewed journals,formulated J&K - Comprehensive State Agriculture Plan (c-SAP) and Carrier advance scheme for SKUAST-K Scientists and teachers association, besides conducted various SKUAST-K initiated livilihood studies in isolated areas of the state.Dr. Wani is twice recipient of DST SERB(GoI), prestigious International Travel Grant Award.

Vegetable Science for Competitive Examinations

Baseerat Afroza
Syed Berjes Zehra
Asima Amin
Ummyiah Masoodi
Gazala Nazir
Shabir A. Wani

NIPA® GENX ELECTRONIC RESOURCES & SOLUTIONS P. LTD.
New Delhi-110 034

NIPA® GENX ELECTRONIC RESOURCES & SOLUTIONS P. LTD.

101,103, Vikas Surya Plaza, CU Block
L.S.C.Market, Pitam Pura, New Delhi-110 034
Ph : +91 11 27341616, 27341717, 27341718
E-mail: newindiapublishingagency@gmail.com
www: www.nipabooks.com

For customer assistance, please contact
Phone: + 91-11-27 34 17 17
Fax: + 91-11- 27 34 16 16

ISBN: 978-93-58879-12-4

Composed and Designed by NIPA®.

Sher-e-Kashmir University of Agricultural Sciences & Technology of Kashmir
Shalimar, Srinagar-190025, J&K India
www.skuastkashmir.ac.in

Prof. Nazir A. Ganai
Vice-Chancellor

Foreword

It is a great pleasure that Division of Vegetable Science, Faculty of Horticulture SKUAST-K has compiled a comprehensive collection of multiple choice questions on various spheres of Vegetable Science. The compilation is expected to be a vital resource for aspirants of various competitive examinations including JRF/SRF/ICAR-NET. This book, meticulously curated and thoughtfully organized, demonstrates the dedicated efforts of authors for nurturing the next generation of experts and leaders in vegetable sciences. Designed to challenge and inspire, the multiple-choice questions contained within this volume cover all the aspects of vegetable production technology and the ever-evolving techniques in modern horticulture. I appreciate the faculty members and contributors who have crafted these questions ensuring that each query serves as a stepping stone towards a deeper appreciation of the intricate interplay between theory and practical application in the realm of vegetable sciences. Hope this book serve as guiding light for all those aspirants embarking on a quest for knowledge, and may it inspire a new generation to make meaningful contributions to the advancement of horticultural sciences. I compliment Prof. S.A. Wani, Dean, Faculty of Horticulture and Dr. Baseerat Afroza Prof. & Head, Division of Vegetable Science and her team of scientists taking this initiative of compiling valuable information in the form of a question bank.

(Nazir Ahmad Ganai)

Place: Shalimar, Srinagar
Dated: 02.12.2023

Shalimar, Srinagar-190025, J&K India
Phone: (Office) 0194-2464028; Fax: 0194-246160 (Resid.) 0194-2463655, 2461543
e-mail: vc@skuastkashmir.ac.in

Preface

This collection of multiple-choice questions has been meticulously curated to offer a comprehensive understanding of the diverse aspects of vegetable sciences. The field of vegetable sciences encompasses the study of various aspects of vegetable production, including cultivation, breeding, physiology, seed production and organic production. This compilation consists of multiple choice questions along with answer keys on different aspects of vegetable science and aims to serve as a valuable resource for students preparing for NET/JFF/SRF and other competitive exams. The questions included herein cover a wide spectrum of topics, ranging from production technology basis up to sustainable agricultural practices. As such, readers will not only enhance their theoretical understanding but also gain practical insights into the real-world applications of vegetable sciences. We extend our appreciations to all the scientists who compiled the questions on different spheres of vegetable science as an informative learning tool for student community.

Authors

Contents

1

Production Technology of Cole Crops

1 *Brassica oleracea* L. var. *botrytis* is the botanical name of

a) Cabbage
c) Cauliflower
b) Knol-Khol
d) None of these

2 Cauliflower was introduced in India in 1822 by ________ from Garden, London.

a) Dr. Jemson
b) Dr. Kalloo
c) Herbalist Dodens
d) None of these

3 Pusa Hybrid-2 is the first F_1 hybrid of cauliflower released by _______ organization.

a) Public sector
b) Private sector
c) Both
d) None of these

4 Pusa Himjyoti is the only variety which may be grown aduring ______ in the hills.

a) Aug-Sep
b) Sep-Oct
c) April-July
d) None of these

5 When tropical cultivars of cauliflower are grown at lower temperature, they produce small size curds. This is commonly termed as

a) Bolting
b) Buttoning
c) Both
d) None of these

6 Seed rate (g/ha) of cauliflower is

a) 400-500
b) 500-600
c) 600-700
d) None of these

7 Pusa Katki and Pusa Deepali are the improved varieties of

a) Cauliflower
b) Cabbage
c) Chinese cabbage
d) None of these

8 Seed rate (g/ha) of cabbage is

a) 300-400 b) 400-500

c) 500-600 d) None of these

9 Botanical name of red cabbage is

a) *Brassica oleracea* var. *capitata* b) *Brassica oleracea* var.*rubra*

c) *Brassica oleracea* var.*sylvestris* d) None of these

10 *Brassica oleracea* var. *capitata* is the botanical name of

a) Cabbage b) Red cabbage

c) Cauliflower d) None of these

11 Cabbage has anti-cancer property due to

a) Indole-2-carbinol b) Indole-2 butaric

c) Indole-3-carbinol d) None of these

12 Cabbage belongs to family

a) *Cruciferae* b) *Cucurbitaceae*

c) Both d) None of these

13 *Brassica oleracea* var.*sylvestris* is also known as

a) Field cabbage b) Wild cabbage

c) Both d) None of these

14 *Brassica oleracea* var.*sylvestris* is also known as

a) Cliff cabbage b) Colewort

c) Both d) None of these

15 Cabbage bears seed in special kind of bicarpellary fruit which is called

a) Pod b) Bud

c) Siliqua d) None of these

16 Cultivated cabbage is

a) Perennial b) Biennial

c) Both d) None of these

17 Wild cabbage is

a) Perennial b) Biennial

c) Both d) None of these

18 *Brassica oleracea* var. *sabauda* is the botanical name of

a) White cabbage b) Red cabbage
c) Savoy cabbage d) None of these

19 Self-incompatibility is found in

a) Cauliflower b) Pea
c) Cabbage d) None of these

20 The flowers of cabbage are

a) Protandrous b) Protogynous
c) Both d) None of these

21 The number of days taken by early group of cabbage to reach edible stage is

a) 40-50 b) 55-70
c) 70-90 d) None of these

22 Black leg is the major disease of

a) Cauliflower b) Cabbage
c) Both d) None of these

23 *Phoma lingum* resistant variety of cabbage is

a) Early Drum Head b) Pusa Drum Head
c) Late Drum Head d) None of these

24 First tropical variety of cabbage is

a) Pusa Ageti b) Pusa Sambandh
c) Both d) None of these

25 Black leg disease of cabbage is caused by

a) *Phoma sylivistis* b) *Phoma lingum*
c) *Phoma chinensis* d) None of these

26 Cabbage variety which can be cultivated under high temperature conditions is

a) Pusa Drum Head b) Pusa Ageti
c) Pusa Sambandh d) None of these

27 Cabbage grown in saline soils is more susceptible to disease

a) Hollow heart b) Black-neck
c) Black-leg d) None of these

28 Cabbage produces seed only in

a) Tropical areas
b) Temperate areas
c) Sub-tropical areas
d) None of these

29 Pusa Sambandh is a synthetic variety of

a) Cauliflower
b) Cabbage
c) Chinese cabbage
d) None of these

30 The conditions where the seed of Pusa Ageti can be produced are

a) Tropical areas
b) Sub-tropical areas
c) Temperate areas
d) None of these

31 Cabbage maybe grown almost throughout the year in

a) Mid hills
b) Southern hills
c) Both
d) None of these

32 Cabbage seedlings become Lanky due to the over dose of

a) Phosphorous
b) Nitrogen
c) Calcium
d) Sulphur

33 Cabbage seedlings are transplanted at

a) 2-4 true leaf stage
b) 4-6 true leaf stage
c) 6-8 true leaf stage
d) None of these

34 Black rot resistant variety of cabbage is

a) Pride of India
b) Golden Acre
c) Pusa Mukta
d) Copen Hagen Market

35 *Brassica oleracea* var. *gongyloides* or caulorapa is the botanical name of

a) Cabbage
b) Cauliflower
c) Knol-Khol
d) None of these

36 Knol-Khol is also called as

a) Broccoli
b) Kohlrabi
c) Both
d) None of these

37 Seed rate (g/ha) of Kohlrabi is

a) 400-500
b) 500-600
c) 600-700
d) 1000-1500

38 The inflorescence in Knol-Khol is

a) Cymose
b) Racemose
c) Both
d) None of these

39 Sporophytic self – incompatibility is found in

a) Cabbage
b) Knol-Khol
c) Both
d) None of these

40 Edible part of Knol-Khol is

a) Root
b) Leaves
c) Swollen stem
d) None of these

41 Chinese cabbage is grown as pot herb and also as

a) Leafy crop
b) Salad crop
c) Bulb crop
d) None of these

42 Genetic male sterility has been reported in broccoli by

a) Alter (1959)
b) Cole (1959)
c) Both
d) None of these

43 The country with largest production of Broccoli in the world is

a) China
b) U.S.A.
c) India
d) None of these

44 White Vienna and King of Market are improved varieties of

a) Knol-Khol
b) Cabbage
c) Cauliflower
d) Broccoli

45 Palam Samridhi is an improved variety of

a) Broccoli
b) Cabbage
c) Cauliflower
d) Chinese cabbage

46 Brussels sprouts is a

a) Cool crop
b) Moisture loving crop
c) Both
d) None of these

47 *Brassica oleracea* var.*acephala* is the botanical name of

a) Cabbage
b) Kale
c) Broccoli
d) None of these

48 Dania is a variety of

a) Cabbage
b) Cauliflower
c) Knol-Khol
d) None of these

49 Chromosome number in Chinese cabbage is

a) 2n = 18
b) 2n = 20
c) 2n = 24
d) None of these

50 The type of incompatibility in broccoli is

a) Gametophytic
b) Sporophytic
c) Both
d) None of these

51 Brussels sprouts is also known as

a) Sprouts
b) Buttons
c) Mini cabbage
d) All the above

52 Which of the following varieties of cauliflower is self blanching type?

a) Pant Shunhra
b) Snow Ball-16
c) Hissar
d) Pusa Ketki

53 Vegetable crops belonging to the cole crops thrive best in

a) Cool weather
b) Hot humid climate
c) Arid climate
d) Semi-arid climate

54 White Vienna is _________ season variety of Knol-khol

a) Early
b) Mid
c) Late
d) All season

55 Whiptail in cauliflower is caused by

a) Excess of boron
b) Deficiency of boron
c) Excess of molybdenum
d) Deficiency of molybdenum

56 Fleshy edible part of knol-khol is an enlargement of

a) Root
b) Stem
c) Leaf
d) None of these

57 Early Cauliflower is ready for harvesting in the period of

a) Mid Sep to mid-Nov
b) Mid-Nov to mid-Jan
c) Mid Jan to April
d) None of these

58 Hardening of cabbage seedlings may be done by with-holding irrigation prior to transplanting

a) 4-6 days b) 6-8 days

c) 8-10 days d) 10-12 days

59 Healthy and stocky seedlings of cauliflower are transplanted

a) 60 × 30-45cm b) 60 ×60 cm

c) 45 ×45 cm d) 40 ×15 cm

60 The most nutritive type of broccoli is

a) Purple coloured b) White coloured

c) Green coloured d) None of these

61 The first synthetic cabbage variety was recommended in the year

a) 1990 b) 1991

c) 1992 d) 1993

62 Browning in cauliflower can be corrected by the application of

a) Ammonium molybdenum b) Boric acid

c) Zinc sulphate d) Urea

63 The best suited soil pH range for cauliflower is

a) 5.5-6.5 b) 6.5-7.5

c) 7.5-8.5 d) 6.0-7.0

64 When the surface of curd in cauliflower is loose and has velvety appearance then it is called

a) Fuzziness b) Blindness

c) Riciness d) Browning

65 All cole crops have developed from wild cabbage known as

a) Cole-wart b) Cole-sprout

c) Cole-coli d) None of these

66 Early cauliflower varieties are available for consumption in

a) Dec-Jan b) Mid Sep-mid-Oct

c) Jan-Feb d) March-April

67 Mid-season cauliflower varieties are available for consumption in

a) Mid-Nov to mid-Dec b) Mid Sep to mid Oct

c) Mid Jan to mid -Feb d) April to May

68 Which one of the following is a cole crop?

a) Beet root b) Turnip

c) Knol-Khol d) Spinach

69 Isolation distance of cabbage for foundation seed production is

a) 800 m b) 1000 m

c) 1600 m d) None of these

70 Riciness in cauliflower is due to

a) High temperature b) Low temperature

c) Both d) None of these

71 Indian cauliflower is tolerant to

a) Low temperature b) High temperature

c) Both d) None of these

72 The edible portion of cabbage is

a) Leaf b) Head

c) Root d) Stem

73 Kunwari is the variety of

a) Knol-Khol b) Cabbage

c) Cauliflower d) None of these

74 The seed required for growing seedlings for planting in one hectare area of Knol-khol is

a) 500-800g b) 900-1000 g

c) 1000-1500 g d) None of these

75 The place of origin of sprouting broccoli is

a) Italy b) India

c) America d) None of these

76 Brussels sprouts matures in

a) 90-100 days b) 60-80 days

c) 120-180 days d) 40-60 days

77 The center of origin of cauliflower is

a) Germany b) France

c) Greece d) Cyperus

78 Blindness in cauliflower is due to

a) Excess of nitrogen
b) Nitrogen deficiency
c) Insect injury to terminal bud
d) High temperature

79 Which of the cauliflower requires chilling temperature for seed production?

a) Pusa Deepali
b) Pusa Synthetic
c) Pusa Shubhra
d) None of these

80 Late cauliflower does not set seed in plains due to absence of

a) Long day and high temperature
b) Long day
c) Short day and high temperature
d) Short day and low temperature

81 Pusa Mukta , an improved variety of cabbage is resistant to

a) White rot
b) Black rot
c) Downy mildew
d) Powdry mildew

82 Cabbage is cross pollinated owing to

a) Floral morphology
b) Protandry
c) Self-incompatibility
d) None of these

83 Bt cabbage is resistant to

a) DMB
b) Cabbage butterflies
c) Aphid
d) Painted bug

84 The cauliflower mosaic virus particles contain

a) RNA
b) DNA
c) Both
d) None of these

85 Cross pollination in cabbage is due to

a) Floral structure
b) Protandry
c) Protogyny
d) Self-incompatibility

86 Hollow stem of cauliflower is due to deficiency of

a) Boron
b) Zinc
c) Molybdenum
d) Copper

87 Seed rate of sprouting broccoli (g/ha) is

a) 150-250
b) 350-400
c) 500-600
d) 700-800

88 Among the following European vegetables which one is rich source of protein?

a) Broccoli
b) Brussels
c) Kale
d) Red cabbage

89 Flat head or drum head and savoy types of cabbage cultivars have _______ maturity.

a) Early type
b) Mid type
c) Late type
d) None of these

90 Chromosome number in cauliflower is

a) 2n = 18
b) 2n=20
c) 2n = 24
d) None of these

91 Chinese cabbage originated from hybridization between turnip and

a) Kole
b) Chinese cabbage
c) Both
d) None of these

92 Chinese sarson No-1 is __________ type of chinese cabbage

a) Heading
b) Non-heading
c) Both
d) None of these

93 Brassica oleracea var. italica is the botanical name of

a) Chinese cabbage
b) White cabbage
c) Cabbage
d) Broccoli

94 Edible part of broccoli is

a) Green buds
b) Thick fleshy floral stalk
c) Both
d) None of these

95 Sprouting broccoli is the richest source of

a) Sulphoraphane
b) Sulpharadene
c) Both
d) None of these

96 Kale is propogated through

a) Seed
b) Vegetable
c) Both
d) None of these

97 Karam Sag and Dwarf Green Curled Scotch are the improved varieties of

a) Cabbage
b) Kale
c) Cauliflower
d) None of these

98 Sporophytic self incompatibility is found in

a) Broccoli b) Brussels sprouts

c) Knol-Khol d) All the above

99 Dania is a variety of

a) Cabbage b) Cauliflower

c) Knol-khol d) None of these

100 Which of the following is the early variety of cabbage?

a) Pride of India b) Early Drum Head

c) Chieftain d) None of these

Answer Key

1	b	2	a	3	a	4	c	5	b	6	a	7	a
8	c	9	b	10	a	11	a	12	a	13	b	14	c
15	c	16	b	17	b	18	c	19	c	20	b	21	b
22	b	23	b	24	b	25	a	26	b	27	b	28	b
29	c	30	b	31	c	32	b	33	b	34	c	35	c
36	c	37	d	38	b	39	b	40	c	41	b	42	b
43	b	44	a	45	a	46	c	47	b	48	a	49	b
50	d	51	d	52	b	53	a	54	a	55	d	56	b
57	a	58	a	59	a	60	c	61	c	62	b	63	d
64	a	65	a	66	b	67	a	68	c	69	c	70	b
71	b	72	b	73	c	74	c	75	a	76	a	77	d
78	c	79	c	80	d	81	b	82	c	83	a	84	b
85	d	86	a	87	b	88	c	89	c	90	a	91	b
92	b	93	b	94	c	95	a	96	a	97	b	98	d
99	a	100	a										

2

Production Technology of Cucurbits

1 Which soil is most suitable for bottle gourd cultivation?

a) Sandy loam soils.
b) Clayey soil
c) Clayey loam soil
d) Silt loam soil

2 The ideal pHof soil for growing bottle gourdis?

a) 4-5
b) 8-9
c) 3-4
d) 6-7

3 What is the desirable soil temperature for good bottle gourd growth?

a) 35-40°C
b) 10-15°C
c) 18°-22°C
d) 40-45°C

4 Which soils are most suitable for growing bitter gourd?

a) Sandy loam and silt loam soils
b) Clay soil
c) Sandy soil
d) Clayey loam soil

5 Optimum pH range for growing bitter gourdis?

a) 6.5-7.0
b) 4-5
c) 7-8
d) 9-12

6 Which is the favourable temperature for cultivation of squash?

a) 10-20°C
b) < 10°C
c) 24-28°C
d) 40-45°C

7 What is the recommended soil for growing squash?

a) Clayey soil
b) Sandy loam soil
c) Silt loam soil
d) Clayey loams oil

8 Can we grow cucumberin winter?

a) No, it is very susceptible to frost injury
b) Yes
c) Yes sometimes
d) None ofthe above

9 What is the optimum temperature for growth incucumber?

a) 18-24°C b) 6-7°C

c) 35-40°C d) >40

10 What is the ideal pH of soil for cucumber cultivation?

a) 7-8 b) 4-5

c) <4 d) 6-7

11 In what type of soil Cucumber growsvery well?

a) Sandy loamy b) Clayey soil

c) Silt loam soil d) Clayey loam soil

12 What is the optimum temperature for good storage lif eof cucumber?

a) >40°C b) 25°C

c) 10°C d) 30°C

13 Bottle gourd ismostly sown by which method?

a) Broadcasting b) Line sowing

c) Dibbling d) Furrow Method

14 The depth of furrows for sowing of bottle gourd should be?

a) 10 cm b) 5-6 m

c) 4 m d) 2-3 m

15 How many times the field is ploughed before sowing of bitter gourd?.

a) 2 times b) 5-6 times

c) 1 time d) 3-4 times

16 What is the seed rate of cucumber?

a) 1 Kg b) 1.5 Kg

c) 2.5-4 Kg d) 1.5 Kg

17 Can direct sowing be practiced in bitter gourd?

a) Yes b) No

c) Only direct sowing can be done d) None ofthe above

18 When is the optimum sowing time for squash cultivation?

a) Mid April – May b) Dec-jan

c) Aug-Sept d) Jan - Feb

19 How much is there commended spacing for squash?

a) 2 m
b) 50 cm
c) 70 cm
d) 100 cm x 75-100 cm

20 When is harvesting done in squash?

a) Fruits are harvested when they attain a desirable size but still tender
b) When fully mature
c) When rind becomes hard
d) When fruit colour changes

21 When to follow intercultural operations in squash?

a) Regularly
b) One month interval
c) 1week interval
d) Only once

22 Name the Pre-emergence herbicide used in cucumber?

a) Paraquat
b) Fluchloralin
c) Atrazine
d) 2,4 D

23 What is the plantto plant spacing of cucumber?

a) 60-90 cm
b) 30-40 cm
c) 20-25cm
d) 10-20 cm

24 How much irrigation water is applied in squash?

a) Irrigation is given at weekly intervals
b) At monthly interval
c) At 2 day interval
d) Only once

25 What isthe sowing time of cucumber in hills?

a) Dec-Jan
b) Aug-Sept
c) Jan – Feb
d) April-may

26 Application of which growth regulator increases the number of flowers & fruit setting in cucumber ?

a) Ethrel
b) Abscicic acid
c) GA
d) Silver nitrate

27 Name two growth regulators used to induce male flowers on gynoecious cucumber.

a) GA (1500-2000 ppm) & Silvernitrate [200-300 ppm]
b) Ethrel & GA

c) Abscicicacid & Silvernitrate

d) Auxin & GA

28 What is the Optimum length of the fruit in cucumber (cm)at edible maturing stage?

a) 10 cm | b) <10 cm
c) 20-25 cm | d) 15 cm

29 What is the maturity index [colour] in salad or slicing cucumber?

a) White spine colour | b) Yellow spine colour
c) Green spine colour | d) Brown spine colour

30 What is the optimum yield in t/haunder green house conditions using tropical gynoecious hybrids ofcucumber

a) 200t/ha | b) 50t/ha
c) 100t/ha | d) 25t/ha

31 For transportation how are cucumber spacked?

a) Gunny bags | b) Wooden boxes
c) Polythene bags | d) Baskets

32 Which physiological storage disorder is observed when fruits in cucumber are exposed to temperature below 10°C for prolonged period?

a) Chilling injury | b) Pillow
c) Bottleneck | d) Leaf silvering

33 How much FYM should be applied at the time of last ploughing in case of bitter gourd?

a) 10-15 tonnes | b) 7-8 tonnes
c) 15-20 tonnes | d) 20-25 tonnes

34 What is the NPK requirement cucumber per ha?

a) 1.50:50:50 Kg | b) 70:50:25 Kg
c) 120:80:60 Kg | d) 100:75:50 Kg

35 Is nursery raising feasible for growing bottle gourd crop?

a) Yes, it can be sownin poly bags

b) Only nursery raising is practiced

c) Only direct sowing is practiced

d) Both b & c

36 Seedlings of bottle gourd are transplanted after how many days of sowing?

a) 40 days b) 1 week

c) 2 months d) 15-20 days

37 What is the optimum temperature for sowing bottle gourd under protected conditions?

a) >30°C b) 15-18°C

c) 20°C d) 35-40

38 Under protected conditions, how are seeds of bottle gourd generally sown?

a) Poly bags c) Directly in soil

c) In fiber bags d) None of the above

39 Is it possible to sow bitter gourd seeds in polybags?

a) Yes b) No

c) Can only be sown directly in field d) None of the above

40 When are the seeds of bitter gourd sown in polybags under Kashmir conditions?

a) Dec b) Oct

c) April d) june

41 Germination period under protected conditions for bitter gourd depends on what conditions?

a) The right temperature and humidity

b) Right temperature ony

c) Right humidity only

d) None of the above

42 After how many days seedlings grown in polybags of bitter gourd can be shifted to pits in the main field?

a) 30-35 days b) 15-20 days

c) 60 days d) 120 days

43 What is the average daily temperature most favourable for raising cucurbitaceous vegetables

a) 10-15°C b) >40°C

c) 30-35°C d) 24-28°C

44 Which soils are best for cultivation of cucurbit?

a) Clayey soil
b) Sandy loam soil
c) Silt loam soil
d) Clayey loam soil

45 Land is prepared for growing cucurbits by?

a) 3-4 ploughings
b) 5-6 ploughings
c) 2 ploughings
d) 1 ploughings

46 How many seeds are sown at one place?

a) 2-3 seeds
b) 10 seeds
c) 1 seed
d) 5-6 seeds

47 When do we transplant seeds in open fields?

a) When the outside temperature rises (May), the seedlings are transplanted in the open fields
b) When the outside temperature falls (May), the seedlings are transplanted in the open fields
c) When the outside temperature rises (June), the seedlings are transplanted in the open fields
d) None ofthese

48 Sex in pumpkin is?

a) Monoecious
b) Dioecious
c) Hermaphrodite
d) None of the above

49 Which chemical is used to induce pistillate flowers in pumpkin?

a) CCC
b) Morphactin
c) Ethepon
d) All of the above

50 What is the recommended seed rate for bottle gourd?

a) 3-7kg/ha
b) 4-8kg/ha
c) 6-8kg/ha
d) 10-12 kg/ha

51 When is sowingof bottle gourd done in open fields?

a) June-July
b) March–April
c) Sept-Oct
d) Mid April-May

52 What is the recommended spacing in bottle gourd?

a) 300 cm × 50 cm
b) 100 cm × 100 cm
c) 200 cm × 100 cm
d) 200-250 cm × 100 cm

53 Summer squash is also called as?

a) Vegetable marrow
b) Summer pepo
c) Karela
d) None of the above

54 Among the cross pollinated vegetables, inbreeding depression is low in?

a) Bulb crops
b) Cole crops
c) Cucurbits
d) Root crops

55 What is the recommended seed rate of cucumber?

a) 1.0 kg/ha
b) 1.5 kg/ha
c) 0.5 kg/ha
d) 2.5kg /ha

56 What is the exact spacing between any two hybrids of cucumber?

a) 100 cm x 50 cm
b) 150 cm x 60 cm
c) 150 cm x 50 cm
d) 250 cm x 50 cm

57 How much is the recommended seed rate of cucumber hybrids?

a) 1-2 kg/ha
b) 1-1.5 kg/ha
c) 1.2-1 kg/ha
d) 1.2-1.5 kg/h

58 What is the spacing between cucumber varieties?

a) 120x30 cm
b) 150x30cm
c) 120x50 cm
d) 160x30cm

59 How is the fruit of ridge gourd and sponge gourd?

a) The fruits of sponge gourd are smooth and possess sharp ridges
b) The fruits of ridge gourd are smooth and possess sharp ridges
c) The fruits of sponge gourd are smooth
d) None of these

60 Which recommended varieties are for Kashmir region in ridge gourd and spongegourd?

a) Pusa chikni
b) Pusa Nasdar
c) Both A and B
d) None of the above

61 What is the recommended seed rate in ridge gourd and sponge gourd?

a) 1.5 kg/ha
b) 5.0 kg/ha
c) 2.0 kg/ha
d) 2.5 kg/ha

62 What is the recommended spacing between ridge gourd and sponge gourd?

a) 150 cm x 50 cm b) 100 cm x 50 cm

c) 100 cm x 60 cm d) 150 cm x 70 cm

63 Short days induce which flowers in ash gourd?

a) Male b) Bisexual

c) Female d) All of the above

64 Which recommended variety of bitter gourd is grown in Kashmir?

a) PusaVishesh b) Pusa Do Mausami

c) Arka Harit d) All of the above

65 Pointed gourd is a perennial crop and it is propagated by?

a) Seeds b) Stem cuttings

c) Root cuttings d) Air layering

66 How many seeds of bitter gourd are sown per hill?

a) 5-7 seeds/hill b) 1-3 seeds/hill

c) 6-10 seeds/hill d) 2-3 seeds/hill

67 What is the recommended seed rate of bitter gourd?

a) 5-6 Kg/ha b) 7-8 Kg/ha

c) 9-10 Kg/ha d) D. 3-4 kg/ha

68 What is the recommended spacing between any varieties in bitter gourd?

a) 150-200 cm x 60 cm b) 100-200 cm x 60 cm

c) 150-250 cm x 60 cm d) 150-200 cm x 60 cm

69 The botanical name of pointed gourd is?

a) *T. dioica* b) *T. cucurmerina*

c) *T. angunia* d) None ofthese

70 Which is the recommended variety of Musk melon for cultivation?

a) Pusa Sharbati b) Hara Madhu

c) Durgapura Madhu d) Afghan Selection

71 What is the recommended seed rate of musk melon?

a) 6-7 kg/ha b) 8-9 kg/ha

c) 4-5 kg/ha d) 9-10 kg/ha

72 What is the sowing time for musk melon?

a) MidApril-May b) April-May

c) May-June d) March-April

73 What is the recommended spacing between any varieties of musk melon?

a) 100 cm x 100 cm b) 100 cm x 150 cm

c) 150 cm x 100 cm d) 150 cm x 200 cm

74 The fruits of pointed gourd are harvested when the seeds are at which stage?

a) Immature b) Germinated

c) Fully matured d) Physiological maturity

75 What is the recommended seed rate of pumpkin?

a) 6 kg/ha b) 7 kg/ha

c) 8 kg/ha d) 9 kg/ha

76 What is the recommended spacing between any two varieties in pumpkin?

a) 200 cm x 75-100 cm b) 300 cm x 100 cm

c) 300 cm x75-100 cm d) 400 cm x75-100 cm

77 Among the cucurbits the longest fruit is found in?

a) Bottle gourd b) Snake gourd

c) Long melon d) Cucumber

78 What isthe recommended seed rate of squash?

a) 3-5 kg/ha b) 7-8kg/ha

c) 10-11kg/ha d) 8-10 kg/ha

79 What is the recommended spacing between varieties in squash?

a) 100 cm x 75-100 cm b) 100 cm x 100 cm

c) 150 cm x 75-100 cm d) 200 cm x 75-100 cm

80 Replanting in pointed gourd is done after how many years?

a) 1 - 2 b) 5 - 7

c) 9 - 10 d) 12 - 15

81 What is the recommended seed rate in water melon?

a) 5-6 kg/ha b) 5-6 kg/ha

c) 3-4 kg/ha d) 8-9 kg/ha

82 What is the sowing time for watermelon?

a) Last week of May b) First week of April

c) Last week of March d) Last week of April

83 What is the recommended spacing in watermelon?

a) 300 cm x 100 cm b) 200 cm x 100 cm

c) 150 cm x 150 cm d) 250 cm x150 cm

84 Chromosome number of bitter gourd is?

a) 22 b) 24

c) 56 d) 84

85 What is the optimum temperature of soil for raising cucurbits?

a) 20-25°C b) 30-35°C

c) 20-24°C d) 24-27°C

86 What is to be done for increasing yield in cucurbits?

a) Hand pollination b) Foliar application of sulphur

c) Foliar application of boron d) Noneofthese

87 Which cucurbit is a perennial, dioecious and possess a tuberous root?

a) Bitter gourd b) Sweet gourd

c) Pumpkin d) Tinda

88 Which is a mutant variety of bitter gourd?

a) CO.1 b) Preethi

c) MDU1 d) Arka Harit

89 Sweet gourd is propagated through?

a) Seeds b) Stem nodes

c) Tuberous roots d) Petioles

90 Which cucurbits are trained via *pandal* system?

a) Bitter gourd b) Snake gourd

c) Ridge gourd d) All of the above

91 Bitter taste in bitter gourd is due to an alkaloid called?

a) Cucurbitacin b) Momorcidin

c) Charantian d) Noneofthe above

92 Super long variety of ridge gourd?

a) CO.1 b) CO.2

c) Pusa Chikini d) Arka Nasdar

93 Variety of ridge gourd moderately resistant to downy mildew?

a) Arka Nasdar b) Pusa Nasdar

c) Arka Sujat d) CO.1

94 Which disease mostly effects pumpkin and squash?

a) Downy mildew b) Alternaria leaf spot

c) Powdery mildew d) None of these

95 Which diseases mostly effects bottle gourd?

a) Alternaria Leaf spot b) Powdery mildew.

c) Both A and B d) None of the above

96 Which crops are not raised in onesingle plot?

a) Sponge gourd and ridge gourd

b) Muskmelon, long melon and snap melon

c) Pumpkin and squash

d) All of above

97 Which soils are not favorable for cultivation of cucurbits?

a) Heavier b) Wet and poorly drained soils

c) Both A and B d) None of these

98 Most drought hardy crop in cucurbits?

a) Pumpkin b) Bottle gourd

c) Cucumber d) Ridge gourd

99 The systems of planting incucurbits are?

a) Pits b) Bed

c) Ridges and furrows d) All of the above

100 After drying which vegetable is used as domestic utensils?

a) Pumpkin b) Cucumber

c) Bottle gourd d) Ridge gourd

101 Edible part of pumpkin is ?

a) Endocarp b) Pericarp

c) Mesocarp d) All of the above

102 Which variety of pumpkin is rich in carotene content?

a) Arka chandan
b) Arka harit
c) Pusa do Mausami
d) Arka Vishesh

103 Maturity indices for harvesting wax gourd is?

a) Wine drying
b) Petiole drying
c) Appearance of ashy bloom
d) Disappearance of ashy bloom

104 A species of Momordica which is called as balsam apple?

a) *M. cochichinensis*
b) *M. cymbalaria*
c) *M. charantia*
d) *M. balsimina*

105 High temperature during early vegetative phase of ridge gourd increases the production of which type of flowers?

a) Male
b) Bisexual
c) Female
d) All of the above

106 Average yield of ridge gourd in tones from 1 ha is?

a) 5 - 10
b) 15 - 20
c) 25 - 30
d) > 25

107 Average number of fruits per plant in sponge gourd varies from?

a) 5 - 10
b) 10 - 15
c) 15 - 20
d) 20 - 30

108 Edible part of ribbed gourd/sponge gourd and ash gourd is?

a) Endocarp
b) Pericarp
c) Mesocarp
d) Exocarp

109 Origin of bottle gourd is?

a) Asia
b) India
c) Java
d) Europe

110 Cucurbits exhibit phyto-toxic effects due to spray of ?

a) Sulphur
b) Copper
c) Both
d) None of the above

111 Botanical name of pickling cucumber/West Indian Gherkin?

a) *Cucumis anguria*
b) *Cucumis longipes*
c) *Cucumis longipes* var. *longipes*
d) *Cucumis longipes* var. *anguria*

112 Musk melon can tolerate?

a) Slight acidity
b) Slight alkalinity
c) High acidity
d) High alkalinity

113 Musk melon is which type of fruit?

a) Climateric
b) Non climateric
c) Semi- climateric
d) None of these

114 A melon which is suitable for growing in both tropical and sub-tropical climates?

a) Snap melon
b) Long melon
c) Musk melon
d) Netted melon

115 Among the cucurbits which records the highest iron content?

a) Water melon
b) Musk melon
c) Gherkin
d) Cucumber

116 Tinda is native of?

a) Tropical Africa
b) India
c) Tropical America
d) Ethiopia

117 The area where cucurbits are grown in river beds/river basins are called as?

a) Waste lands
b) Deserts
c) Diara lands
d) Dry lands

118 River bed system of planting is also a form of?

a) Vegetable forcing
b) Relay cropping
c) Sequential cropping
d) Vegetable enforcing

119 The main breeding objective in cucumber is to breed which lines?

a) Monoecious
b) Dioecious
c) Andromonoecious
d) Gynoecious

120 Calypso is a hybrid of ?

a) Cucumber
b) Gherkin
c) Summer squash
d) Winter squash

121 Example of single seeded berry?

a) Coccinia
b) Sweet gourd
c) Pointed gourd
d) Chow chow

122 Chow chow is propogated through?

a) Whole fruit b) Stem cuttings

c) Root cuttings d) Budding

123 Which cucurbit exhibit viviparous nature of seed?

a) Pumpkin b) Chow chow

c) Snap melon d) Pointed gourd

124 Semi-perennial cucurbits?

a) Ivy gourd b) Chow chow

c) Both d) None of the above

125 In India, cucumber is mainly used as?

a) Cooking vegetable b) Pickle

c) Dessert d) Salad

Answer Key

1	a	2	d	3	c	4	a	5	a	6	c	7	b
8	a	9	a	10	d	11	a	12	c	13	d	14	d
15	d	16	c	17	a	18	a	19	d	20	a	21	a
22	b	23	a	24	a	25	d	26	a	27	a	28	c
29	a	30	a	31	d	32	a	33	d	34	d	35	d
36	d	37	b	38	a	39	a	40	c	41	a	42	a
43	d	44	b	45	a	46	a	47	a	48	a	49	d
50	c	51	d	52	d	53	a	54	c	55	d	56	c
57	d	58	a	59	a	60	c	61	d	62	a	63	c
64	c	65	b	66	d	67	a	68	a	69	a	70	d
71	c	72	a	73	c	74	a	75	a	76	c	77	b
78	b	79	a	80	c	81	c	82	d	83	b	84	a
85	a	86	a	87	b	88	c	89	c	90	d	91	b
92	b	93	c	94	c	95	c	96	d	97	c	98	b
99	d	100	c	101	b	102	a	103	c	104	d	105	a
106	b	107	c	108	a	109	b	110	c	111	a	112	a
113	a	114	b	115	a	116	b	117	c	118	a	119	d
120	b	121	d	122	a	123	b	124	c	125	d		

3

Production Technology of Root Crops

1 What is the main negative impact of physiological disorders on root crops?

a) Deterioration of quality and visual characteristics

b) Nutritional imbalance

c) Decrease in yield

d) None of these

2 Forking is a common physiological disorder of which root crop?

a) Radish b) Carrot

c) Beetroot d) Turnip

3 Akashin, a common physiological disorder of Radish is caused by?

a) Boron deficiency and low day and night temperature

b) Boron deficiency and high day and night temperature

c) Calcium deficiency and low day and night temperature

d) Calcium deficiency and high day and night temperature

4 Brown heart of turnip can be managed by?

a) Borax @ 10-15kg/ha

b) Copper oxychloride @ 0.3%

c) Manganese sulphate @ 10-15kg/ha

d) Carbendazim @ 3kg/ha

5 Which physiological disorder leads to the development of pores in radish root?

a) Cavity spot b) Brown heart

c) Pithiness or pore extent d) Forking

6 Deficiency of Calcium causes which physiological disorder in Carrot?

a) Brown heart b) Forking

c) Water core d) Cavity spot

7 What is the major symptom associated with Cavity spot disorder of Carrot?

a) Collapsing of the root epidermis forming a cavity

b) Development of pores

c) Root cracking or splitting

d) All of these

8 Root splitting or cracking is mainly caused by?

a) Nutritional imbalance

b) High rainfall

c) Frost

d) Long period of dry weather followed by sudden wet weather

9 What are the major physiological disorders that affect Turnip crop?

a) Cavity spot

b) Water core

c) Brown heart

d) Both b and c

10 Pungency is a physiological disorder of which root crop?

a) Turnip

b) Radish

c) Carrot

d) Beetroot

11 Leaf blight of carrot is more predominant in which season?

a) Summer season

b) Rainy season

c) Winter season

d) All of these

12 Turnip Yellow Mosaic Virus is mainly transmitted by?

a) Flea beetle

b) Aphids

c) White fly

d) None of these

13 Which physiological disorder of turnip is mainly prevalent in acidic soil?

a) Water core

b) Brown heart

c) Forking

d) Browning

14 The development of Damping off disease in root crops is favoured by?

a) Excessive application of fertilizers

b) Dry weather

c) Excessive soil moisture

d) High pH

15 Mottling of leaves and development of chlorotic ring spots is the most common symptom of?

a) Aster yellows
b) Damping off
c) Beet yellowing virus
d) Bacterial leaf blight

16 Speckled yellows disorder of beetroot is caused by?

a) Deficiency of manganese
b) Deficiency of boron
c) Deficiency of calcium
d) None of these

17 Speckled yellows disorder of beetroot can be corrected by the application of?

a) Calcium sulphate @ 10-15kg/ha
b) Borax @ 10-15kg/ha
c) Manganese sulphate @ 10-15kg/ha
d) Copper oxychloride @ 10-15kg/ha

18 Which variety of Radish is resistant to forking?

a) Pusa Gulabi
b) Pusa Shweta
c) Pusa Chetki
d) Punjab Safed

19 Kalyanpuri No. 1 variety of radish shows resistance to which disease?

a) Bacterial leaf blight
b) White rust
c) Cercospora leaf spot
d) Bacterial leaf spot

20 What is the main reason for the development of pithiness in radish roots?

a) Delayed harvesting
b) Deficiency of nitrogen
c) Water logging
d) Nutritional imbalance

21 Which fungicides are mainly recommended for the control of White Rust disease of Radish?

a) Carbendazim @3kg/kg of seed
b) Copper oxychloride @0.3%
c) Mancozeb @10kg/ha
d) Both a and b

22 Seed treatment with Thiram 75 WP or Captan 50 WP is effective for prevention of which major disease of Radish and Carrot?

a) Bacterial leaf spot
b) Aster yellows
c) Alternaria blight
d) Bacterial leaf blight

23 Incidence of bolting is less in which variety of Carrot?

a) Pusa Meghali
b) Pusa Kesar
c) Pusa Vrishti
d) Early Nantes

24 Leaf spot is a widespread disease of which root crop?

a) Carrot b) Turnip

c) Beetroot d) Radish

25 What are the important cultural practices recommended for the control of leaf spot disease in carrot?

a) Crop rotation and field sanitation b) Mulching

c) Tillage d) Removal of weeds

26 Which disease gives a "Witches' Broom" appearance to the carrot tops?

a) Black root rot b) Sclerotinia rot

c) Carrot yellows d) Common scab

27 Cracking of carrot roots can be prevented by?

a) Maintenance of optimum moisture in the field

b) Harvesting crop at right maturity stage

c) Supply of recommended doses of N

d) All of these

28 What is the most special feature of Pusa Kanchan variety of Turnip?

a) Its roots do not develop pithiness even if harvesting is delayed

b) It is resistant to cercospora leaf spot

c) Both a and b

d) It is best for dehydration

29 Delayed harvesting in case of Turnip generally leads to?

a) Pungency b) Both c and d

c) Development of bitterness d) Coarse texture

30 Which disease of root crops facilitates secondary bacterial infections?

a) Dry rot b) Soft rot

c) Both a and b d) Cercospora leaf spot

31 Which Physiological disorder leads to the appearance of grey or brown colour in the inner portion of turnip roots?

a) Water core b) Brown heart

c) Both a and b d) Cavity spot

32 Inner portion of the roots becomes soft and mushy due to the attack of which disease?

a) Common scab b) White rust

c) Soft rot d) Both b and c

33 How does Akashin disorder affect the radish crop?

a) It checks the root growth b) It affects the colour of root

c) It increases pungency d) None of these

34 Alternate dark and light-coloured rings on the root are the symptoms of which physiological disorder?

a) Cavity spot b) Browning

c) Water core d) Zoning

35 Beet Yellowing Virus is transmitted by?

a) White fly b) Aphids

c) Flea bettle d) Thrips

36 What is the best way to manage bacterial blight of eetroot?

a) Use of clean & disease-free seed b) Use of Bactericides

c) Mulching d) None of these

37 The main symptom associated with Beet Curly Top Virus is?

a) Development of leaf spots

b) Development of hairy root appearance

c) Root splitting

d) None of these

38 Cercospora leaf spot of beetroot is caused by?

a) Bacteria b) Virus

c) Fungus d) Nematode

39 Which is one of the most serious diseases of carrot both in the field and storage?

a) Bacterial leaf blight b) Bacterial soft rot

c) Cercospora leaf spot d) Common scab

40 What are the most damaging foliar diseases of carrot?

a) Alternaria b) Cercospora

c) Bacterial leaf blight d) All of these

41 *Alternaria raphani* infection in radish is mainly characterised by development of?

a) Small, yellowish slightly raised lesions on the leaves

b) Root cracking and splitting

c) Curling of leaves

d) None of these

42 Which disease affects the leaves and flowering shoots of radish?

a) Common scab b) Aster yellows

c) White rust d) Cavity spot

43 What causes black spots in Turnip leaves?

a) *Alternaria raphanin* b) *Alternaria brassicola*

c) *Alternaria brassicae* d) Both b and c

44 Powdery mildew diseases of root crops can be controlled by the application of which fungicides?

a) Dinocap b) Wettable sulphur

c) Both a and b d) None of these

45 How can we manage the viral diseases of root crops?

a) Destruction of infected plants

b) Field sanitation

c) Use of resistant varieties and management of vector population

d) All of these

46 Which disease causes the development of small reddish orange spots on Beet leaves?

a) White rust b) Beet rust

c) Damping off d) Root rot

47 Enlargement of secondary root growth causes which disorder in carrot and radish?

a) Cavity spot b) Pithiness

c) Forking d) Cracking

48 What kind of varieties in case of root crops tend to split more?

a) Late varieties b) Early varieties

c) Both a and b d) None of these

49 Which disorder leads to the development of hollow cavity inside turnip roots?

a) Water core
b) Zoning
c) Hollow heart
d) Pithiness

50 Which variety of Beetroot shows less symptoms of boron deficiency?

a) Crimson Globe
b) Early Wonder
c) Long Dark Blood
d) Detroit Dark Red

51 Which is the most favourable climate in which almost all root crops can be grown?

a) Humid
b) Hot
c) Cool
d) All of these

52 Which chemical is used for pre-sowing treatment in carrot?

a) Thiram
b) Carbendazim
c) Mancozeb
d) Copper sulphate

53 An important operation to be done after germination of seeds of root crops to keep proper distance between plants is?

a) Mulching
b) Weeding
c) Thinning
d) Hoeing

54 Which of the following is not a variety of carrot?

a) Chamman
b) Local Black
c) Early Nantes
d) Pusa Desi

55 Sowing time of Carrot is?

a) January-February
b) March-April
c) August-September
d) November-December

56 What is the recommended spacing followed in carrot?

a) 30 cm x 15 cm
b) 15 cm x 15 cm
c) 45 cm x 30 cm
d) 60 cm x 45 cm

57 What is the recommended dose of manure for carrot production?

a) FYM@ 20-25 t/ha
b) Cow dung @ 15t/ha
c) FYM@ 50t/ha
d) All of these

58 Red round is a variety of which root crop?

a) Beetroot
b) Radish
c) Carrot
d) Turnip

59 What is the recommended dose of fertilizers for production of carrot?

a) N:P:K @ 90:60:60 kg/ha b) N:P:K @ 10:10:10 kg/ha

c) N:P:K @ 20:40:60 kg/ha d) N:P:K @ 45:25:20 kg/ha

60 What quantity of vermicompost is sufficient for the better root yield in carrot?

a) 2t/ha b) 10t/ha

c) 30t/ha d) 25t/ha

61 Radish is sown in the month of?

a) January b) March

c) August d) December

62 What is the seed rate of radish?

a) 10-20 kg/ha b) 2-3 kg/ha

c) 25-35 kg/ha d) 7.5-10 kg/ha

63 What is the recommended spacing followed for sowing radish?

a) 30 cm x 15-20 cm b) 45 cm x 15 cm

c) 25 cm x 25-30 cm d) 60 cm x 45 cm

64 What is the recommended dose of manure for radish production?

a) FYM@ 20-25 t/ha b) FYM @ 15-20 t/ha

c) FYM@ 50t/ha d) FYM @ 5t/ha

65 What is the recommended dose of fertilizers for production of radish?

a) N:P:K @ 90:60:60 kg/ha b) N:P:K @ 30:10:20 kg/ha

c) N:P:K @ 20:50:60 kg/ha d) N:P:K @ 55:25:20 kg/ha

66 Which of the following varieties of radish is used for table purpose?

a) Scarlet Globe b) Punjab Safed

c) Pusa Chetki d) Pusa Reshmi

67 What is the sowing time of radish for table purpose?

a) January-February b) December-January

c) March-June d) July-August

68 What is the seed rate of radish for table purpose?

a) 2-4 kg/ha b) 8-10 kg/ha

c) 15-18 kg/ha d) 20-25 kg/ha

69 What is the recommended spacing of radish for table purpose?

a) 20 cm x 5-10 cm b) 35 cm x 15 cm

c) 25 cm x 25-30 cm d) 60 cm x 40 cm

70 What is the recommended dose of manure for table purpose in radish?

a) FYM@ 20-25 t/ha b) FYM @ 15-20 t/ha

c) FYM@ 50t/ha d) FYM @ 5t/ha

71 What is the recommended dose of fertilizers for table purpose in production of radish?

a) N:P:K @ 80:60:60 kg/ha b) N:P:K @ 30:10:20 kg/ha

c) N:P:K @ 20:50:60 kg/ha d) N:P:K @ 50:25:25 kg/ha

72 Which of the following is a variety of turnip?

a) Nageen-1 b) Pusa Shewta

c) Pusa Jamuni d) Chamman

73 What is the sowing time of turnip?

a) January-February b) August-September

c) November-December d) March-April

74 What is the seed rate of turnip?

a) 2-3 kg/ha b) 5-7 kg/ha

c) 10-15 kg/ha d) 25-30 kg/ha

75 What is the recommended spacing for turnip?

a) 20 cm x 5-10 cm b) 35 cm x 15 cm

c) 30 cm x 15-20 cm d) 60 cm x 40 cm

76 What is the recommended dose of manure for turnip production?

a) FYM@ 20-25 t/ha b) FYM @ 15-20 t/ha

c) FYM@ 40t/ha d) FYM @ 35t/ha

77 What is the recommended dose of fertilizers for production of turnip?

a) N:P:K @ 80:60:60 kg/ha b) N:P:K @ 30:10:20 kg/ha

c) N:P:K @ 90:90:60 kg/ha d) N:P:K @ 50:25:25 kg/ha

78 Which of the following is not a variety of beetroot?

a) Crimson Globe b) Detroit Dark Red

c) Pusa Jamuni d) Early Eonder

79 What is the sowing time of beetrrot?

a) January-February b) August-September

c) November-December d) March-April

80 What is the seed rate of beetroot?

a) 2-3 kg/ha b) 5-7 kg/ha

c) 10-12 kg/ha d) 25-30 kg/ha

81 What is the recommended spacing for beetroot?

a) 20 cm x 5-10 cm b) 35 cm x 15 cm

c) 30 cm x 15-20 cm d) 60 cm x 40 cm

82 What is the recommended dose of manure for beetroot production?

a) FYM@ 20-25 t/ha b) FYM @ 15-20 t/ha

c) FYM@ 60t/ha d) FYM @ 55t/ha

83 What is the recommended dose of fertilizers for production of beetroot?

a) N:P:K @ 80:60:60 kg/ha b) N:P:K @ 30:10:20 kg/ha

c) N:P:K @ 90:80:60 kg/ha d) N:P:K @ 75:50:60 kg/ha

84 Which of the following is not a variety of carrot?

a) Chamman b) Early Nantes

c) Pusa Rudhira d) Early Wonder

85 Recommended variety of radish for seed production is?

a) Japenese White Long b) Pusa Vasuda

c) White Round d) Both a and c

86 Recommended variety of turnip for seed production is?

a) Purple Top White Globe b) Nageen

c) Pusa Asita d) Both a and b

87 Which is the best method of seed production in case of root crops?

a) Seed to seed method b) Head to seed method

c) Root to seed method d) All of these

88 When are the roots of turnip uprooted for replanting for seed production?

a) January b) March

c) June d) November

89 What is the spacing for seed production in root crops?

a) 60 cm x 40 cm
b) 60 cm x 30 cm
c) 45 cm x 40 cm
d) 30 cm x 20 cm

90 What is the isolation distance in carrot for foundation and certified seeds?

a) 1000 m and 700 m
b) 500 m and 450 m
c) 1000 m and 800 m
d) 900 m and 500 m

91 What is the isolation distance in radish for foundation and certified seeds?

a) 1000 m and 600 m
b) 1500 m and 1000 m
c) 1000 m and 700 m
d) 900 m and 500 m

92 What is recommended dosage of manure for seed production of root crops?

a) FYM@ 20-25 t/ha
b) FYM @ 15-20 t/ha
c) FYM@ 60t/ha
d) FYM @ 55t/ha

93 What is the recommended dose of fertilizers for seed production of root crops?

a) N:P:K @ 85:60:60 kg/ha
b) N:P:K @ 120:90:60 kg/ha
c) N:P:K @ 90:80:60 kg/ha
d) N:P:K @ 70:50:60 kg/ha

94 Which colour of umbel indicate perfect time for seed extraction in case of carrot?

a) Yellow
b) Green
c) Purple
d) Brown

95 Which are the poor quality umbels?

a) Primary umbels
b) Lower umbels
c) Secondary umbels
d) Both a and c

96 What is the curing time of harvested root plants for proper storage?

a) 8 days
b) 7 days
c) 12 days
d) 5 days

97 Moisture level to be present in dried seeds of root crops is?

a) 10%
b) 12-15%
c) 20%
d) 8%

98 What is the depth of trenches in which stecklings of root crops are kept for overwintering?

a) 5ft b) 4ft

c) 3ft d) 2ft

99 The native place of carrot is?

a) Central Asia b) Mediterranean region

c) Tropical Africa d) None of these

100 Which state is famous for carrot in India?

a) Karnataka b) Rajasthan

c) Haryana d) Goa

Answer Key

1	a	2	b	3	b	4	a	5	c	6	d	7	a
8	d	9	d	10	b	11	c	12	a	13	b	14	c
15	c	16	a	17	c	18	d	19	b	20	a	21	d
22	c	23	b	24	a	25	a	26	c	27	d	28	a
29	b	30	c	31	b	32	c	33	a	34	d	35	b
36	a	37	b	38	c	39	b	40	d	41	a	42	c
43	d	44	c	45	d	46	b	47	c	48	b	49	c
50	d	51	c	52	a	53	c	54	d	55	c	56	a
57	a	58	b	59	a	60	b	61	c	62	d	63	a
64	b	65	a	66	a	67	c	68	b	69	a	70	b
71	d	72	a	73	b	74	b	75	c	76	b	77	c
78	c	79	b	80	c	81	c	82	a	83	d	84	d
85	d	86	d	87	c	88	d	89	b	90	c	91	b
92	b	93	b	94	d	95	b	96	b	97	b	98	d
99	a	100	c										

4

Production Technology of Bulb Crops

1 What is the best time to sow onion seeds in Northern Hilly regions?

a) January to February b) March to April

c) May to June d) September to November

2 Which type of soil is best for onion cultivation?

a) Sandy loam b) Clay loam

c) Alluvial soil d) Both a and b

3 What should be the pH range for onion cultivation?

a) 4.4-5.0 b) 5.5-6.5

c) 6.0-7.5 d) 6.5-7.5

4 What should be the height of onion seedlings at the time of transplanting?

a) 15-20 cm b) 6-8 cm

c) 25-35 cm d) None of these

5 What are the common pests that affect onion crop?

a) Trips b) Onion maggots

c) Cutworms d) All of these

6 How long does it take for onion crop to mature?

a) 90-95 days b) 100-110 days

c) 120-150 days d) 165-170 days

7 Purple blotch of onion is caused by?

a) *Alternaria porri* b) *Alternaria solani*

c) *Alternaria dauci* d) *Alternaria raphanin*

8 White rot of onion is caused by?

a) Bacteria b) Virus

c) Fungus d) Nematode

9 What is the recommended fertilizer application for onion crop?

a) 60-80 kg N, 50-60 kg PO5 and 60-70 kg KO per hectare

b) 25-30 kg N, 30-40 kg PO5 and 50-60 kg KO per hectare

c) 40-60 kg N, 30-50 kg PO5 and 50-80 kg KO per hectare

d) 75-80 kg N, 60-70 kg PO5 and 50-60 kg KO per hectare

10 What is the average yield of onion crop?

a) 10-15 t/ha b) 15-20 t/ha

c) 20-25 t/ha d) 25-30 t/ha

11 What are the maturity indices for harvesting onion?

a) 20-30% neckfall stage b) 35-40% neckfall stage

c) 50-70% neckfall stage d) None of these

12 Onion is left for drying for how many days after harvesting?

a) 5-7 days b) 10-12 days

c) 15-20 days d) 28-30 days

13 Which of the following is not a variety of onion?

a) Agrifound Light Red b) Agrifound Dark Red

c) Pusa Rudhira d) Punjab Naroya

14 Pusa Red is a variety of?

a) Garlic b) Leek

c) Onion d) Shallot

15 What is the recommended spacing for onion plants?

a) 15-20 cm x 8-12 cm b) 25-35 cm x 15-25 cm

c) 45-50 cm x 30-40 cm d) None of these

16 What is the average yield per acre for onion?

a) 5-7 tonnes b) 8-10 tonnes

c) 15-20 tonnes d) 25-35 tonnes

17 What is the ideal temperature range for onion cultivation?

a) 5-10 °C b) 15-25 °C

c) 20-30 °C d) 35-40 °C

18 How long does it take for onions to germinate after planting?

a) 5-6 days b) 7-10 days

c) 15-20 days d) 20-25 days

19 How many onion seedlings should be planted per acre?

a) 1000-5000 b) 12000-18000

c) 250000-300000 d) 400000-500000

20 How long can onions be stored under temperate conditions?

a) 2-3 months b) 6-8 months

c) 10-15 months d) 1 year

21 What is the recommended packaging material for onions in temperate conditions?

a) Mesh bags b) Woven sacks

c) Polythene bags d) Both a and b

22 How do you prevent sprouting in stored onions?

a) Captan b) Mancozeb

c) Thiram d) Maleic hydrazide

23 What is the optimum storage temperature to prevent sprouting in stored onions?

a) 5-10 °C b) 4-5 °C

c) 2-3 °C d) 0-1 °C

24 Red Globe variety of onion is suitable for?

a) Cooking b) Processing

c) Seed production d) None of these

25 Irrigation in onion should be given at what intervals?

a) 2-5 days b) 6-7 days

c) 10-15 days d) 20-25 days

26 What is the best time to plant garlic in Northern hills?

a) March-April b) May-June

c) August-September d) October-November

27 What is the ideal soil type for garlic cultivation?

a) Alluvial soil b) Clayey soil

c) Loamy soil d) All of these

28 What is the ideal pH for garlic cultivation?

a) 4.5-5.5 b) 5.0-6.0

c) 6.0-7.0 d) 6.5-7.5

29 What is the ideal temperature for garlic growth?

a) 5-7 °C b) 8-10 °C

c) 10-20 °C d) 20-25 °C

30 How is garlic propagated?

a) Seeds b) Leaves

c) Cuttings d) Cloves

31 At the time of harvesting, the colour of garlic leaves change to?

a) Dark green b) Yellow

c) Purple d) Black

32 How long can garlic be stored under temperate conditions?

a) 1-2 months b) 4-5 months

c) 6-8 months d) 10-12 months

33 Which soils are detrimental for Pran cultivation?

a) Light soils b) Heavy soils

c) Both a and b d) None of these

34 Pran is propagated through?

a) Cloves b) Bulbs

c) Bulbils d) Both b and c

35 How many weedings are to be done during the growth period of Pran?

a) 1 b) 2

c) 3 d) 4

36 How many days before, the irrigation is to be stopped before harvesting of the Pran?

a) 5-7 days b) 10-12 days

c) 15-20 days d) 20-25 days

37 What are the two main categories of Pran?

a) Green shallots and yellow shallots

b) Grey shallots and pink shallots

c) Dark green shallots and pink shall ts

d) Yellow shallots and grey shallots

38 What is the most common harvest maturity of Pran?

a) Size of plant b) Texture of bulb

c) Bulb diameter d) Both a and c

39 How many seasons are required for the seed production in Pran?

a) 1 b) 2

c) 3 d) 4

40 The outer skin colour in onion is due to?

a) Anthocyanin b) Lycopene

c) Quercetin d) Xanthophyll

41 Where is the biggest onion market in India located?

a) Karnataka b) Rajasthan

c) Punjab d) Maharashtra

42 What is the average yield of Shallot?

a) 5-6 t/acre b) 7-8 t/acre

c) 9-12 t/acre d) 15-20 t/acre

43 What is the optimum size of garlic cloves for planting?

a) 4-5 mm b) 5-7 mm

c) 6-7 mm d) 8-10 mm

44 Which bulb crop has highest nutritive value?

a) Leek b) Shallot

c) Garlic d) Pran

45 What is the ideal spacing for pran cultivation?

a) 20 cm × 15 cm b) 15 cm × 15 cm

c) 15 cm × 10 cm d) 10 cm × 8 cm

46 What should be the colour of onion seeds at the time of seed harvesting?

a) Yellow b) Brown

c) Black d) Purple

47 Onion belongs to which family?

a) Lilliaceae b) Compositae

c) Alliaceae d) Brassicaceae

48 What is the scientific name of leek?

a) *Allium cepa* b) *Allium sativum*

c) *Allium porum* d) None of these

49 What is the origin of garlic?

a) Tropical Africa b) Sri Lanka

c) Indo-Burma d) Central Asia

50 What is the chromosome number of leek?

a) 16 b) 18

c) 24 d) 32

51 Which acid is present in onion?

a) Citric acid b) Malic acid

c) Tartaric acid d) None of these

52 Aroma in onion is due to the presence of?

a) Dimethyl pyrazine b) Isothiocyanate

c) Nonadienal d) Allyl propyl disulphide

53 Aroma in garlic is due to the presence of?

a) Dimethyl pyrazine b) Isothiocyanate

c) Diallyl disulphide d) Allyl propyl disulphide

54 Male sterility is present in which bulb crop?

a) Leek b) Onion

c) Garlic d) Pran

55 Protoandry is present in which bulb crop?

a) Garlic b) Onion

c) Leek d) Both b and c

56 Onion is a ____________ plant?

a) Day neutral b) Short day

c) Long day d) Both b and c

57 What is the rooting depth of onion?

a) 10-12 cm b) 15-30 cm

c) 20-25 cm d) 30-40 cm

58 Respiration rate of onion is?

a) Very low b) Low

c) Moderate d) High

59 What is the seed rate of garlic?

a) 200 kg/ha b) 300 kg/ha

c) 400 kg/ha d) 500 kg/ha

60 What is the seed rate for rabi onion?

a) 5-7 kg/ha b) 8-9 kg/ha

c) 10-12 kg/ha d) 15-20 kg/ha

61 What is the rank of India in area and production of onion?

a) 1 b) 2

c) 3 d) 4

62 Which type of inflorescence is present in onion?

a) Raceme b) Corymb

c) Umbellate d) Cyme

63 Onion is highly cross pollinated due to which phenomenon?

a) Protogyny b) Protoandry

c) Both a and b d) None of these

64 Arka Lalima is a variety of?

a) Garlic b) Shallot

c) Leek d) Onion

65 Critical day length required for bulbing in garlic is?

a) 10 hours b) 12 hours

c) 14 hours d) 16 hours

66 What is the scientific name of garlic?

a) *Allium cepa* b) *Allium sativum*

c) *Allium porum* d) None of these

67 Allin is present in which bulb crop?

a) Leek b) Shallot

c) Garlic d) Pran

68 Agrifound Parvati is a variety of?

a) Leek b) Onion

c) Garlic d) Pran

69 Garlic is harvested during which month?

a) January-February b) March-April

c) June-July d) November-December

70 Splitting in garlic occurs due to?

a) Excess nitrogen b) Boron deficiency

c) Calcium deficiency d) Delayed harvesting

71 Black mould of onion is caused by?

a) *Alternaria porii* b) *Fusarium oxysporum*

c) *Aspergillus niger* d) *Albugo candida*

72 What is the causal organism of yellow dwarf disease of garlic?

a) *Fusarium oxysporum* b) MLO

c) *Uromyces pisi* d) *Rhizoctonia solani*

73 What is the scientific name of onion fly?

a) *Athalia lunnus* b) *Bemisia tabacii*

c) *Mimegralla coeruleferons* d) *Delia antiqua*

74 Excess moisture and soil moisture causes which physiological disorder in garlic?

a) Black heart b) Hollow heart

c) Pencil strip d) Sprouting

75 Tip burn in bulb crops is caused due to deficiency of?

a) Sulphur b) Boron

c) Calcium d) Magnesium

76 What is the chromosome number of onion?

a) 12 b) 16

c) 20 d) 32

77 Onion is a rich source of?

a) Vitamin A b) Vitamin B

c) Vitamin C d) None of these

78 Red colour in onion is due to?

a) Anthocyanin
b) Lycopene
c) Quercetin
d) Xanthophyll

79 ICAR-Directorate on Onion and Garlic research is located at?

a) Delhi
b) Maharashtra
c) Pune
d) Bangalore

80 Onion and Garlic is stored at a RH of?

a) 40-50%
b) 60-70%
c) 80-90%
d) 85-98%

81 Important pest of onion is?

a) *Athalia lunnus*
b) *Bemisia tabacii*
c) *Earias vitelli*
d) *Thrips tabacii*

82 Which place in Maharashtra is the biggest onion market in India?

a) Nasik
b) Lassalgoan
c) Panchgani
d) Ratnagiri

83 Which state of India is the highest producer of garlic?

a) Kerela
b) Goa
c) Madhya Pradesh
d) Haryana

84 Which part of garlic is typically used for cooking?

a) Roots
b) Stems
c) Bulbs
d) Flowers

85 What is the name for the process by which garlic's sharp taste and strong smell mellows when cooked?

a) Caramelization
b) Fermentation
c) Hydrolysis
d) Dehydration

86 Which country is the largest producer of garlic?

a) India
b) Korea
c) China
d) Japan

87 Which of the following crop is sexually sterile?

a) Garlic
b) Onion
c) Leek
d) None of these

88 Onion is chiefly pollinated by?

a) Wind b) Thrips
c) Honey bees d) None of these

89 What is the anthesis time in onion?

a) 3-4 am b) 5-9 am
c) 10-11 am d) 3-4 pm

90 What should be the diameter of garlic bulb for export purpose?

a) 10-20 mm b) 20-30 mm
c) 40-60 mm d) None of these

91 Curing is done to remove?

a) Excess nitrogen b) Excess moisture
c) Both a and b d) None of these

92 Which of the following is used to increase bulb size and yield in garlic?

a) Captan b) Thiram
c) Borax d) Maleic hydrazide

93 What is the flower colour of onion?

a) White or bluish b) Yellow
c) Purple d) None of these

94 Which country is the leading exporter of onion in the world?

a) India b) USA
c) China d) Netherlands

95 Optimum temperature for bulb development of onion is?

a) 10-15 °C b) 15-20 °C
c) 20-25 °C d) 25-30 °C

96 What is the scientific name of tree onion?

a) *Allium cepa* b) *Allium cepa var aggregatum*
c) *Allium cepa var viviparum* d) *Allium sativum*

97 What is the common name of *Allium cepa var aggregatum?*

a) Potato onion b) Underground onion
c) Multiplier onion d) All of these

98 Which of the following is a frost hardy crop?

a) Pran b) Garlic

c) Shallot d) None of these

99 G-282 is a variety of?

a) Leek b) Onion

c) Garlic d) Pran

100 Antibacterial substance present in garlic is?

a) Allin b) Allicin

c) Isothiocyanate d) Nonadienal

Answer Key

1	a	2	b	3	b	4	a	5	c	6	d	7	a
8	d	9	d	10	b	11	c	12	a	13	b	14	c
15	c	16	a	17	c	18	d	19	b	20	a	21	d
22	c	23	b	24	a	25	a	26	c	27	d	28	a
29	b	30	c	31	b	32	c	33	a	34	d	35	b
36	a	37	b	38	c	39	b	40	d	41	a	42	c
43	d	44	c	45	d	46	b	47	c	48	b	49	c
50	d	51	c	52	a	53	c	54	d	55	c	56	a
57	a	58	b	59	a	60	b	61	c	62	d	63	a
64	b	65	a	66	a	67	c	68	b	69	a	70	b
71	d	72	a	73	b	74	b	75	c	76	b	77	c
78	c	79	b	80	c	81	c	82	a	83	d	84	d
85	d	86	d	87	c	88	d	89	b	90	c	91	b
92	b	93	b	94	d	95	b	96	b	97	b	98	d
99	a	100	c										

5

Production Technology of Leafy Vegetable Crops

1 The soils best suited for leafy vegetables are:

a) Clayey soils
b) Well drained loamy soils
c) Sandy soils
d) Any type of soil

2 How long does itgenerally take for leafy vegetables to grow?

a) 35-50 days after sowing
b) 100-120 days after sowing
c) 90-95 days after sowing
d) 50-60 days after sowing

3 The cultivation of leafy vegetables is easy during

a) Summer season
b) Winter season
c) Spring season
d) Rainy season

4 What is the fertilizer requirement for coriander?

a) 15:30:15kg/haNPK
b) 20:40:20kg/haNPK
c) 10:30:20kg/haNPK
d) 10:40:20kg/haNPK

5 The chromosome number of *Spinacea oleracea* is:

a) 2n=16
b) 2n=18
c) 2n=12
d) 2n=20

6 The bes tconditions for growth of leafy greens are:

a) Fully shaded
b) Waterlogged
c) Barren
d) Full sun to lightly shaded

7 The most common leafy vegetable grown in India during summer is:

a) Lettuce
b) Amaranthus
c) Spinach
d) Swisschard

8 The cultivation of leafy greens or similar vegetables without soil is called:

a) Tradophonics b) Nutrioponics

c) Hydroponics d) Stratoponics

9 Sun light requirement for leafy vegetables is:

a) 1-2 hours b) 6-8 hours

c) >15 hours d) No light requirement

10 The cultivation of leafy vegetables is considered tobe:

a) Difficult and time-consuming b) Cost ineffective

c) Prone to failures d) Easy and quick

11 Effect of excess heat on the quality of leafy vegetables:

a) Premature yellowing b) Rapid softening

c) Wilting and dehydration d) All of the above

12 The common name of spinach is:

a) Palak b) Saag

c) Patta Gobi d) Dhaniya

13 The ideal temperature range for growing most leafy vegetables is:

a) 30-35°C b) 21-26°C

c) 9-11°C d) 29-37°C

14 The ideal pH range for growing most leafy vegetables is:

a) 5.0to 5.5 b) 8.0-9.0

c) 6.0to 6.5 d) Any pH is feasible

15 Chaulai is the common name of which leafy vegetable?

a) Spinach b) Chinese Cabbage

c) Lettuce d) Amaranthus

16 Jobner Green and Arka Anupama are the varieties of:

a) Palak b) Lettuce

c) Chinese Cabbage d) Kale

17 Bolting in leafy vegetables refers to:

a) Premature defoliation b) Premature flowering

c) Yellowing of leaves d) Dropping of flowers

18 Spinach is a memberof the family:

a) Solanaceae b) Compositae

c) Cruciferae d) Chenopodiaceae

19 4 primary sex forms are seen in:

a) Spinach b) Carrot

c) Lettuce d) Kale

20 Methi is the common name of:

a) Amaranthus b) Fenugreek

c) Lettuce d) Coriander

21 Centre of origin of Lettuceis:

a) India b) Tropical Asia

c) Eastern Mediterranean region d) China

22 Leafy vegetables are generally rich in:

a) Vitamin K b) Proteins

c) Vitamin A d) Carbohydrates

23 Spinach is richin which nutrient?

a) Calcium b) Iron

c) Vitamin C d) Protein

24 Which of the leafy vegetablesis commonly grown in hydroponic systems?

a) Spinach b) Lettuce

c) Kale d) Amaranthus

25 Which of the Indian leafy vegetables is known as"red spinach"?

a) Spinach b) Lettuce

c) Kale d) Amaranthus

26 What is the color of the flowers of a lettuce plant?

a) White b) Pink

c) Yellow d) Purple

27 What is the scientific name of lettuce?

a) Lactuca sativa *b) Coriandrum sativum*

c) *Betavulgaris var.cicla* *d) Amaranthus* spp.

28 Poor man's spinach is the common name of which leafy vegetable?

a) Kale
b) Spinach
c) Mustard greens
d) *Amaranthus* spp.

29 What is the spacing for leaf type amaranthus?

a) 10-15 cm x 20-30 cm
b) 20-30 cm x 10-15 cm
c) 30-40 cm x 20-25 cm
d) 15-20 cm x 30-40 cm

30 When is leaf type amaranthus ready for harvesting?

a) 15-20 days after sowing
b) 20-25days after sowing
c) 25-30 days after sowing
d) 30-35days after sowing

31 Bolting in spinach is caused by:

a) Low temperature and short days
b) High temperature and long days
c) Excessive watering
d) Pest infestation

32 Seed rateof spinach is:

a) 25-35kg/ha
b) 35-45kg/ha
c) 45-55kg/ha
d) 55-65kg/ha

33 What are the two types of amaranthus?

a) Grain type and leaf type
b) Red and green varieties
c) Summer and winter varieties
d) Round and flat leaf varieties

34 What is the leaf yield of amaranthus?

a) 5-7t/ha
b) 7-9t/ha
c) 9-11t/ha
d) 11-13t/ha

35 In hills,spinach is sown during which month?

a) January-April
b) March-June
c) May-August
d) September-December

36 What is the leaf yield of spinach?

a) 50-70 q/ha
b) 70-90 q/ha
c) 90-110q/ha
d) 100-150q/ha

37 What is the sowing time for coriander?

a) January-February and September-October

b) March-April and November-December

c) June-July and October-November

d) July-August and December-January

38 Coriander performs well at a temperature range of:

a) 10-15°C b) 15-20°C

c) 20-25°C d) 25-30°C

39 What is the seed rate of coriander?

a) 5-8 kg/ha (Irrigatedcrop), 10-15 kg/ha (Rainfed crop)

b) 10-12 kg/ha (Irrigatedcrop), 20-25 kg/ha (Rainfedcrop)

c) 15-18 kg/ha (Irrigatedcrop), 25-30 kg/ha (Rainfedcrop)

d) 20-22 kg/ha (Irrigated crop), 30-35 kg/ha (Rainfed crop)

40 First weeding in coriander is done after how many days?

a) 15 days after sowing b) 30 days after sowing

c) 45 days after sowing d) 60 days after sowing

41 What is the leaf yield of coriander?

a) 4-5t/ha b) 5-6t/ha

c) 6-7t/ha d) 7-8t/ha

42 What is the easiest way to cool leafy vegetables?

a) Hydro-cooling b) Refrigeration

c) Freezing d) Air-drying

43 What is the ideal time of day for watering leafy vegetables?

a) Midday b) Early morning

c) Late afternoon d) Evening

44 Can amaranthus be grown throughout the year?

a) No

b) Yes, only under North Indian conditions

c) Yes,only under South Indian conditions

d) Yes, under all Indian conditions

45 Which is the hardiest leafy vegetable?

a) Spinach b) Lettuce

c) Amaranthus d) Kale

46 Average seed rate of Kale is:

a) 300-350g/ha b) 350-400 g/ha

c) 400-450 g/ha d) 450-500 g/ha

47 What is the best planting time in North India for growing kale?

a) August-October b) June-August

c) April-June d) October-December

48 Harvesting period of Kale is:

a) September-November b) November-January

c) February-April d) March-June

49 What is the per hectare yield of Kale?

a) 50-100 quintals b) 100-150 quintals

c) 200-300 quintals d) 100-200 quintals

50 Under protected conditions lettuce can be grown during which season?

a) June to October b) November to March

c) April to July d) August to December

51 What is the seed rate of lettuce?

a) 250-375 gm/ha b) 375-500 gm/ha

c) 500-625 gm/ha d) 625-750 gm/ha

52 How can germination of lettuce seeds be enhanced?

a) Cold stratification

b) Scarification

c) Soaking the seeds in water for16 hours

d) Gibberellic acid treatment

53 What is there commended dose of fertilizers for lettuce?

a) 60:40:40kg NPK/ha b) 50:70:50kg NPK/ha

c) 60:80:60kg NPK/ha d) 70:90:70kg NPK/ha

54 What is the seed rate of fenugreek?

a) 20-25kg/ha b) 35-40kg/ha

c) 30-35kg/ha d) 25-30kg/ha

55 What should be the bed size for sowing fenugreek seeds?

a) 3 m x 2 m b) 3 m x 3 m

c) 4 m x 3 m d) 5 m x 4 m

56 What is the leaf yield off enugreek?

a) 5-6t/ha b) 6-7t/ha

c) 7-8t/ha d) 8-9t/ha

57 Amaranthus is mainly pollinated by:

a) Bees b) Butterflies

c) Hummingbirds d) Wind

58 Which of the following is dioecious in nature?

a) Lettuce b) Spinach

c) Cabbage d) Kale

59 Malabar nightshade is the common name of which leafy vegetable?

a) Lettuce b) Spinach

c) Mustard greens d) Basella

60 Basella can be propagated by:

a) Grafting b) Seeds

c) Stem cutting d) Both b and c

61 Optimum temperature for growing basella is:

a) 25-30°C b) 15-20°C

c) 20-25°C d) 10-15°C

62 What is the scientific name of Swiss chard?

a) *Beta vulgaris var. cicla* b) *Spinacia oleracea*

c) *Brassica oleracea var. acephala* d) *Amaranthus tricolor*

63 Tip burn in lettuce is caused by the deficiency of which nutrient?

a) Nitrogen b) Calcium

c) Magnesium d) Potassium

64 The plant whose leaves are seeds are consumed as cereal is:

a) Fenugreek b) Coriander

c) Amaranthus d) Lettuce

65 Which is the mos twidely cultivated species of Amaranth in India?

a) *Amaranthus cruentus* b) *Amaranthus caudatas*

c) *Amaranthus blitum* d) *Amaranthus tricolor*

66 The anti-nutritional compounds present in Amaranthus are:

a) Oxalates b) Nitrates

c) Phytates d) Both a and b

67 The pollination behaviour observed in Amaranthus is:

a) Grain types cross-pollinated; vegetable types self-pollinated

b) Grain types cross-pollinated; vegetable types cross-pollinated

c) Both types are self-pollinated

d) Both types are cross-pollinated

68 Optimum leaf: stem ratio of amaranthus should be:

a) <1 b) >1

c) =1 d) None of the above

69 Which of the following varieties of Amaranth is tetraploid in nature?

a) CO-1 b) CO-4

c) CO-5 d) CO-2

70 Seed yield of amaranthus is generally:

a) 200 kg/ha b) 500 kg/ha

c) 100 kg/ha d) 350 kg/ha

71 Which of the following vegetables is highly tolerant to saline soils?

a) Lettuce b) Amaranth

c) Basella d) Palak

72 Which sowing method is considered best in case of Indian spinach/ Palak?

a) Broadcasting b) Line sowing

c) Check row planting d) Dibbling

73 Type of fruit in Indian spinach/Palak is:

a) Capsule b) Siliqua

c) Multigerm d) Berry

74 Which of the following is a Palak variety?

a) Pusa Jyoti b) Pusa Bharati

c) Punjab Green d) All of the above

75 Ancestor of Indian spinach/Palakis:

a) *Beta vulgaris var. maritime* b) *Beta vulgaris var. cicla*

c) *Beta vulgaris var. conditiva* d) *Beta vulgaris var. crassa*

76 Palak seeds germinate in about how many days after sowing?

a) 20-25 days b) 8-10 days

c) 2-3 days d) 10-20 days

77 Which of the following vegetables has the highest ORAC Oxygen radical absorbancecapacity)?

a) Lettuce b) Kale

c) Spinach d) Swiss chard

78 Ancestor of Spinach *(Spinacia oleracea)* is:

a) *Spinacia spinosa* b) *Spinacia trifolia*

c) *Spinacia tetrandra* d) *None of the above*

79 Optimum temperature (°C) for the germination of Spinach seeds is:

a) 25-30 b) 6-7

c) 30-40 d) 10-15

80 Khara Lucknowa is a local cultivar of:

a) Spinach b) Lettuce

c) Kale d) Cabbage

81 What are the ideal conditions for the seed production of Spinach?

a) Short days and warm weather b) Long days and cool weather

c) Short days and cool weather d) Long days and warm weather

82 Which of the following vegetables produces prickly seed?

a) Lettuce b) Kale

c) Spinach d) Cabbage

83 Endive and Chicory belong to the family:

a) Chenopodiaeceae b) Cruciferae

c) Umbelliferae d) Asteraceae

84 A common salad vegetable crop, Water cress goes by the scientific name:

a) *Anthriscus cerefolium* b) *Nasturium officinalis*

c) *Lactuca sativa* d) *Cichorium intybus*

85 Progenitor of cultivated lettuce is:

a) *Lactuca serriola* b) *Lactuca virosa*

c) *Lactuca indica* d) *Lactuca iteola*

86 The seeds of which of the following vegetable crops exhibit thermos-dormancy?

a) Chinese cabbage b) Kale

c) Cauliflower d) Lettuce

87 The toxic compound "Lactucopicrin" is found in:

a) Lettuce b) Chicory

c) Cabbage d) Both a and b

88 Big vein of Lettuce, a viral disease is transmitted by:

a) Aphids b) Fungus

c) Thrips d) Leaf hoppers

89 Reskia Wonder, a lettuce cultivar, belongs to the group:

a) Crisp head b) Iceberg

c) Butter head d) Leaf type

90 Russett spotting disorder of lettuce occurs due to:

a) Ethylene injury b) Calcium deficiency

c) Excess of Nitrogen d) Boron deficiency

91 Celery belongs to the family:

a) Compositae b) Cruciferae

c) Chenopodiaceae d) Apiaceae

92 Edible portion of celery is:

a) Seed b) Leaf stalk

c) Flower d) Fruit

93 Florida Golden and Golden are the varieties of:

a) Celery
b) Lettuce
c) Chinese Cabbage
d) Basella

94 Bitterness in celery leaves is mainly caused by:

a) Lowt emperature
b) Excessive fertilizer use
c) High temperature
d) Frequent irrigation

95 Recommended seed rate for Chinese cabbage (transplanting and direct seeding) is:

a) 700 g and 1 kg/ha respectively
b) 500 g and 25 kg/ha respectively
c) 250 g and 500 g/ha respectively
d) 1 kg and 25 kg/ha respectively

96 Chromosome number of Chinese cabbage is:

a) 2n=20
b) 2n=18
c) 2n=24
d) 2n=22

97 Which operation is regarded as the most essential as far as cultivation of lettuce isconcerned?

a) Irrigation
b) Staking
c) Application of growth regulators
d) Mulching

98 Which country is the major producer and exporter of Fenugreek seeds?

a) China
b) Iran
c) India
d) Pakistan

99 "Diosgenin" is produced from the seeds of:

a) Coriander
b) Fenugreek
c) Lettuce
d) Parsley

100 *Trigonella corniculata* is the scientific name of:

a) Kasuri Methi
b) Common Methi
c) Both a and b
d) None of the above

Answer Key

1	b	2	a	3	c	4	d	5	c	6	d	7	c
8	c	9	b	10	d	11	d	12	a	13	b	14	c
15	d	16	a	17	b	18	d	19	a	20	b	21	c
22	??	23	a	24	b	25	c	26	d	27	a	28	b
29	c	30	a	31	d	32	b	33	d	34	a	35	b
36	c	37	a	38	d	39	a	40	b	41	c	42	a
43	d	44	c	45	b	46	a	47	c	48	b	49	a
50	d	51	b	52	c	53	a	54	d	55	a	56	c
57	d	58	b	59	d	60	d	61	a	62	a	63	b
64	c	65	d	66	d	67	a	68	b	69	c	70	a
71	d	72	??	73	a	74	b	75	b	76	d	77	c
78	b	79	a	80	d	81	b	82	c	83	c	84	a
85	d	86	d	87	c	88	b	89	a	90	a	91	b
92	d	93	c	94	c	95	b	96	b	97	a	98	d
99	a	100	d										

6

Production Technology of Solanaceous Crops

1 The best age for transplanting of brinjal seedlings is:

a) 4-5 weeksold b) 1-2 weeksold

c) 8-9 weeksold d) 10-12 weeksold

2 The recommended seed rate of tomato is:

a) 100-200g/ha b) 1-1.2 kg/ha

c) 500-600g/ha d) 33-4 kg/ha

3 The best time for sowing tomato is:

a) September to October b) Mid-March to April

c) Mid-December to January d) August to September

4 Brinjal seedlings are generally grown on?

a) Flat beds b) Sunken beds

c) Raised beds d) None of the above

5 The Brinjal variety which has good cooking quality is:

a) Dilruba b) Arka Neelkant

c) Arka Nidhi d) All of the above

6 The stage of tomato best suited for processing is:

a) Over ripe stage b) Red ripe stage

c) Green mature stage d) Turning stage

7 Optimum seed rate for brinjal varieties (g/ha) is:

a) 500-750 b) 100-200

c) 700-800 d) 1000-15000

8 The best time for transplanting brinjal seedlings is:

a) September- October b) May-June

c) July-August d) March-April

9 Seed rate for raising brinjal hybrids is:

a) 100-200g/ha b) 500-750 g/ha
c) 300-400 g/ha d) 1-1.2 kg/ha

10 The best time for harvesting brinjal crop is:

a) January to February b) March to April
c) May to July d) July to November

11 Fermentation method, alkali method and acid method are common seed extraction methods in:

a) Chilly b) Tomato
c) Brinjal d) Okra

12 Which is best method for extraction of tomato seed?

a) Alkali method b) Fermentation method
c) Acid method d) None of the above

13 The safe moisture percent for storage in tomato is:

a) 6-8% b) 12-15%
c) 10-12% d) 2-3%

14 The spacing needed for raising of brinjal crop is:

a) 75 x 60 cm b) 60 x 45 cm
c) 45 x 45 cm d) 30 x 30 cm

15 The fertilizer requirement for successful cultivation of brinjal is:

a) 120:90:60kg/ha b) 60:60:60 kg/ha
c) 75:75:90 kg/ha d) 120:120:120 kg/ha

16 The optimum depth for sowing of solanaceous seeds in nurseries is:

a) 2-3 mm b) 10-15 mm
c) 24-30 mm d) 5-10 mm

17 The optimum seed rate of chilli crop for one hectare is:

a) 1.5-2.0kg/ha b) 500-600g/ha
c) 4-5kg/ha d) 100-200g/ha

18 The sowing time of chilli is:

a) January to February b) April to May
c) June to August d) September to October

19 The recommended spacing for Shalimar-I tomato is:

a) 60 x 60 cm b) 30 x 30 cm

c) 45 × 30 cm d) 60 x 45 cm

20 The recommended spacing for Roma and Shalimar-II tomato is:

a) 60 x 60 cm b) 30 x 30 cm

c) 90 x 60 cm d) 60 x 45 cm

21 The critical stages for irrigation in chilli crop are:

a) Flowering stage b) Fruit setting stage

c) Fruit picking stage d) Both a and b

22 The pollination behaviour of chilli crop is:

a) Self-pollinated b) Cross-pollinated

c) Often cross-pollinated d) None of the above

23 The fertilizer requirement for successful cultivation of chilli is:

a) 120:80:60kg/ha b) 75:75:75 kg/ha

c) 90:60:60 kg/ha d) 180:120:120 kg/ha

24 Which Brinjal variety is recommended for growing in Jammu & Kashmir?

a) Annamalai b) Pusa Purple Long

c) Pusa purple Cluster d) Mysore Green

25 The scientific name of Brinjal shoot and fruit borer is:

a) Helicoverpa armigera *b) Cestius phycitis*

c) Leucinodes orbonalis *d) Henosepilachna implicta*

26 Catface is a common physiological disorder of:

a) Brinjal b) Okra

c) Potato d) Tomato

27 The recommended dose of NPK for tomato hybrids (kg/ha) is:

a) 150:90: 60 b) 120:60:60

c) 90:90:90 d) 120:120:90

28 What is the harvesting stage of brinjal fruits?

a) When the fruits lose theirs hine

b) When the fruits exhibit glossy appearance

c) When streaks develop on the fruits

d) When the fruits become soft to touch

29 What is the yield of Pusa Purple Long brinjal in one hectare in Jammu & Kashmir?

a) 100-200 kg　　b) 75-150 kg

c) 200-250 kg　　d) 350-300 kg

30 Which variety is recommended for growing in chilli?

a) Kashmir Long-1　　b) Sindhur

c) Pant Abir　　d) Azad Kranti

31 What is the yield of Kashmir Long-1 chilli in one hectare in Jammu & Kashmir?

a) 75 kg　　b) 200 kg

c) 200 kg　　d) 150 kg

32 What is the best season to plant potatoes in Jammu & Kashmir?

a) Summer　　b) Spring

c) Winter　　d) Autumn

33 What are the critical stages for irrigation in potato crop?

a) Tuberization　　b) Bulking

c) Harvesting　　d) Both a and b

34 What should be the size of potato seed for planting?

a) 45 g　　b) 30 g

c) 60 g　　d) 100 g

35 Which chemical can delay sprouting in potato crop?

a) Ethylene　　b) Thiourea

c) Malic hydrazide　　d) GA3

36 What should be the size of sprouts in potato seed crop before planting?

a) 5 cm　　b) 10 cm

c) 1 cm　　d) 3 cm

37 How can sprouting be initiated in potato seed tubers?

a) By dipping seed tubers in 1 ppm of gibberellic acid (1mg/l) for one hour

b) By soaking the seed tubers in HCl for1 hour

c) By spraying the seed tubers with 1% thiourea solution

d) By leaving the tubers out in the sun

38 Which variety of potato is recommended for growing in Jammu & Kashmir?

a) Kufri Jyoti b) Kufri Shailja

c) Kufri Giriraj d) All of the above

39 What is the optimum spacing for potato crop?

a) 60 x 20 cm b) 45 x 45 cm

c) 90 x 60 cm d) 0 x 45 cm

40 Potato crop is ready in how many days?

a) 40-50 days b) 90-120 days

c) 60-90 days d) 180-200 days

41 What is dehaulming in potato?

a) Digging up of potato tubers

b) Removing the sprouts from potato tubers

c) Cutting the foliage above the ground

d) Keeping the harvested tubers in shade

42 At what stage dehaulming is donein potato crop?

a) 15 days before harvesting b) On the day of harvesting

c) 30 days before harvesting d) 7 days after harvesting

43 Greening of potato tubers is due to excess of:

a) Anthocyanins b) Pectin

c) Keratine d) Solanine.

44 What is the best time for potato planting in J&K?

a) September to November b) January to February

c) March to May d) June to August

45 What is the optimum temperature for storing potato tubers?

a) 2to 4°C b) 5-10°C

c) 0°C d) -2°C

46 What is the recommended dose of fertilizers (N: P: K) for potato crop?

a) 150:100:100 kg/ha b) 60:60:60 kg/ha

c) 90:90:60 kg/ha d) 120:90:60 kg/ha

47 Greening of potatoes can be prevented by:

a) Early harvesting
b) Frequent irrigation
c) Earthing up
d) Timely weeding

48 Should we irrigate potato crop after dehaulming?

a) Yes, to encourage further growth
b) No, it may lead to rotting of the tubers
c) Only if there is a prolonged drought
d) It depends on the specific potato variety

49 How do we know that potatoes are ready to harvest?

a) When the leaves start to yellow and die back
b) When the potatoes start to sprout new shoots
c) When the plants reach a certain height
d) When the potatoes are still small and firm

50 What is there commended seed rate for growing potatoes on one hectare?

a) 10-15q/ha
b) 30-40q/ha
c) 50-60 q/ha
d) 20-25 q/ha

51 Second crop of potato in J&K can be grown:

a) After mid-November
b) After mid-July
c) After mid-March
d) Growing 2nd crop is not possible in J&K

52 What are the popular capsicum varieties suitable for cultivation in J&K?

a) California Wonder
b) YoloWonder
c) Nishat-1
d) All of the above

53 How should capsicum be harvested?

a) By pulling them off the plant by hand
b) By using a sharp knife or scissors to cut the stem just above the fruit
c) By shaking the plant to make the fruits fall
d) By using a special capsicum harvesting tool

54 What is the best time to cultivate capsicum in J&K?

a) Winter months (December to February)
b) Spring season (March to May)

c) Summer season (April to October)

d) Monsoon season (July to August)

55 What is the spacing requirement for capsicum plants?

a) Approximately 30 cm apart in rows

b) Approximately 45-60 cm apart in rows

c) Capsicum plants should be planted very close together

d) There is no specific spacing requirement for capsicum

56 How often should capsicum bewatered?

a) Once a month

b) 1-2 times per week, depending on weather conditions and soil moisture

c) Daily

d) Only during flowering

57 How long does it take for capsicum plants to bear fruit?

a) 30-40 days after transplanting

b) 60-80days after transplanting

c) 100-120 days after transplanting

d) Capsicum plants do not bear fruit

58 Largest tomato producing state in India is:

a) Madhya Pradesh b) Karnataka

c) Punjab d) Andhra Pradesh

59 Tangerine colour in tomato is attributed to the presence of:

a) Cis-lycopene b) Lycopene

c) Anthocyanins d) β-carotene

60 Optimum temperature for the production of lycopene in tomato is:

a) 10-15°C b) 21-24°C

c) 25-30°C d) 30-40°C

61 Ancestor of cultivated tomato is:

a) Solanum pimpinellifolium

b) Solanum pennelli

c) Solanum lycopersicum var. cerasiformae

d) Solanum cheesmaniae

62 What is the optimum area needed to raise a tomato nursery?

a) 500 m^2 b) 150 m^2

c) 1000 m^2 d) 250 m^2

63 Pusa Lal Meeruti variety of tomato has been developed through:

a) Mutation breeding b) Selection

c) Hybridisation d) Pedigree method

64 Sodom apple (Progenitor of cultivated brinjal) has the scientific name:

a) *Solanum viarum* b) *Solanum incanum*

c) *Solanum auriculatum* d) *Solanum sisymbrifolium*

65 In brinjal, fruit setting is maximum in:

a) Medium styled flowers b) Short styled flowers

c) Long styled flowers d) Fruit setting is independent of length of style

66 Transgenic brinjal has been developed to provide resistance against which pest?

a) Hadda beetle b) Lacewing bug

c) Fruit and Shoot borer d) Both b and c

67 Planting of which species invicinity of Brinjal aids in pollination?

a) *Tagetes erecta* b) *Anethum graveolens*

c) *Salvia officinalis* d) *Mimosa pudica*

68 Which variety of Brinjal is suitable for ratoon cropping?

a) Hisar Jamuni b) Annamalai

c) Pusa Purple Long d) Arka Neelkanth

69 Most favourable temperature for brinjal production is:

a) 30-35°C b) 21-27°C

c) 16-20°C d) 18-22°C

70 Which type of Brinjal is suited for diabetic patients?

a) Purple b) Dark Green

c) White d) Light Green

71 Green chilli is a rich source of:

a) Capsaicin b) Solanine

c) Diosgenin d) Rutin

72 The most pungent chilli in the world is:

a) Carolina reaper b) Habanero

c) Bhoot Jholakia d) Tabasco

73 The richest vegetable source of thiamine is:

a) Chilli b) Tomato

c) Peas d) Brinjal

74 The seed of chilli remains viable for:

a) 1 year b) 2 years

c) 6 months d) 2 to 3 months

75 Male: Female ratio for seed production in Chilli is:

a) 2:1 b) 1:2

c) 3:1 d) 1:3

76 Average F1 hybrid seed yield in chilli is:

a) 100-150kg/ha b) 500-700 kg/ha

c) 400-500 kg/ha d) 300-350 kg/ha

77 The1st F1 hybrid developed in case of Capsicum crop was:

a) Yolo Wonder b) California Wonder

c) Bharat d) Sweet Banana

78 Which variety of Capsicum is tolerant to bacterial wilt?

a) Bharat b) Arka Gaurav

c) Arka Mohini d) Pusa Deepti

79 Chilli Mosaic Virus (CMV) is transmitted by:

a) Aphids b) White flies

c) Thrips d) Mealy bugs

80 Which variety of Chilli is suitable for colour extraction?

a) Arka Abhir b) Punjab Lal

c) Pusa Jwala d) Both a and b

81 Earthing up in potato is generally done how many days after sowing?

a) 10-15 days b) 35-40 days

c) 50-60 days d) 20-30 days

82 The concept of True Potato Seed (TPS) was given by:

a) Dr. GM Kalloo
b) Dr. Ved Pal Singh
c) Dr. S Ramanujan
d) Pushkarnath

83 Seed rate required for TPS is generally:

a) 200-250g/ha
b) 75-100g/ha
c) 100-120 g/ha
d) 250-400 g/ha

84 Which of the following is a processing variety of potato?

a) Kufri Frysona
b) Kufri Pukhraj
c) Kufri Bahar
d) Kufri Ashoka

85 What is the major problem for potato cultivation in the southern hills?

a) Potato tuber moth
b) Potato scab
c) Black scurf
d) Golden cyst nematode

86 Black heart disorder of potato occurs due to?

a) Excess of N
b) N deficiency
c) Exposure to sunlight
d) Poor ventilation

87 Tomato fruit firmness is determined by:

a) Penetrometer
b) Barometer
c) Durometer
d) Thermometer

88 Who is the father of tomato breeding?

a) Luther Burbank
b) C.M Rick
c) Janaki Ammal
d) Goutham Kallo

89 Optimum temperature for pollination in tomato is:

a) 21°C
b) 27°C
c) 30°C
d) 35°C

90 S-12 variety of tomato is an X-ray induced mutant of which variety?

a) Sioux
b) Roma
c) Pusa Red Plum
d) Marglobe

91 Triple disease resistant variety of tomato is:

a) Pusa Ruby
b) Arka Samrat
c) Arka Rakshak
d) Pusa Sheetal

92 Parthenocarpy in Brinjal is expressed only under:

a) Warm weather conditions
b) High light intensity
c) Absence of irrigation
c) Cold conditions

93 Bitternessin brinjal is due to the presence of:

a) Solanine
b) Polyphenol oxidase
c) Solasodine
d) All of the above

94 Processing cultivars of Brinjal need to possess which major characteristic?

a) Low level of phenolics
b) High dry matter content
c) Both a and b
d) None of the above

95 Which of the following *Capsicum* species is resistant to anthracnose disease?

a) *C. pubescens*
b) *C. baccatum*
c) *C. annum*
d) *C. caedensii*

96 Red colour and Pungency of chilli are mainly attributed to the presence of:

a) Capsaicin and capsanthin respectively
b) Capsanthin and capsaicin respectively
c) Capsaicin only
d) Capsanthin only

97 100 Kg of ripe chilli fruits give______ kg of dry chilli?

a) 25to 40
b) 80 to 100
c) 10 to 20
d) 50 to 75

98 MDU-1 variety of Chilli is?

a) X-ray induced mutant of K-1
b) Gamma ray induced mutant of G-2
c) Spontaneous mutant from Pant C-1
d) Gamma ray induced mutant of K-1

99 What is the critical level of aphid infestation in potato?

a) 20 aphids per 100 compound leaves
b) 20 aphids per 1000 compound leaves
c) 10 aphids per 200 compound leaves
d) 100 aphids per 2000 compound leaves

100 Which of the following varieties of potato are highly resistant to late blight disease?

a) Kufri Girdhari
b) Kufri Himsona
c) Kufri Anand
d) All of the above

Answer Key

1	a	2	c	3	b	4	c	5	d	6	a	7	a
8	b	9	c	10	d	11	b	12	a	13	c	14	b
15	a	16	d	17	a	18	b	19	c	20	d	21	d
22	c	23	a	24	b	25	c	26	d	27	a	28	b
29	c	30	a	31	d	32	b	33	d	34	ab	35	c
36	c	37	a	38	d	39	a	40	b	41	c	42	a
43	d	44	c	45	b	46	a	47	c	48	b	49	a
50	d	51	b	52	d	53	b	54	c	55	b	56	b
57	b	58	d	59	a	60	b	61	c	62	d	63	a
64	b	65	c	66	c	67	d	68	a	69	b	70	c
71	d	72	c	73	a	74	b	75	b	76	d	77	c
78	b	79	a	80	d	81	b	82	c	83	c	84	a
85	d	86	d	87	c	88	b	89	a	90	a	91	b
92	d	93	c	94	c	95	b	96	b	97	a	98	d
99	a	100	d										

7

Production Technology of Leguminous Vegetables

1. Chromosome number of garden pea is
   a) 2n=2x=14   a) 2n=2x=18
   c) 2n=2x=20   b) 2n=2x=22
2. Origin of French Bean
   a) South America   b) South Mexica
   c) Africa   d) Europe
3. Pea is the
   a) Cross-pollinated   b) Often-cross pollinated
   c) Self-pollinated   d) None of the above
4. Shelling percentage of pea is
   a) 23-30%   b) 26-33%
   c) 40-50%   d) 35-45%
5. Contender variety of French Bean is introduced from
   a) Mexico   b) USA
   c) Sweden   d) America
6. Pea variety suitable for dehydration
   a) Arkel   b) Meteor
   c) Wando   d) Lincoln
7. Seed rate of Indian Bean
   a) 10-20kg/ha   b) 50-60kg/ha
   c) 20-30kg/ha   d) 22-40kg/ha
8. Cluster Bean is
   a) Long day plant   b) Short day plant
   c) Day neutral   d) None of the above

9 Largest Cluster Bean growing state

a) Andhra Pradesh | b) Madhya Pradesh
c) Punjab | d) Rajasthan

10 Average heat units time for pea

a) 4.4°C | b) 5.8°C
c) 6°C | d) 3°C

11 Progenitor of French Bean

a) *Phaseolus acutifolius* | b) *Phaseolus polystachyus*
c) *Phaseolus aborigineus* | d) *Phaseolus angularis*

12 Seed rate of bush type French Bean

a) 45kg/ha | b) 70kg/ha
c) 23kg/ha | d) 65kg/ha

13 Limiting amino acid in hyacinth bean

a) Methionine | b) lysine
c) Proline | d) None of the above

14 Botanical name of cow pea

a) *Pisum sativum* | b) *Phaseolus vulgaris*
c) *Lablab purpureus* | d) *vigna unguiculata*

15 French Bean variety resistant to anthracnose

a) Kentucky wonder | b) Tweed wonder
c) TKD-1 | d) SVM-1

16 Among pole types, most commonly grown French bean variety in India

a) Tweed wonder | b) Arka komal
c) Kentucky wonder | d) Pusa parvati

17 Optimum temperature for pea seed germination is about

a) 22°C | b) 24°C
c) 30°C | d) 21°C

18 Origin of Broad bean

a) India | b) Africa
c) America | d) Europe and Asia

19 What is the required temperature for hot water treatment?

a) 30°C b) 50°C

c) 45°C d) 40°C

20 God sent vegetable is

a) French bean b) Broad Bean

c) Winged bean d) Indian Bean

21 Origin of Cowpea

a) Central Asia b) Central Africa

c) Mexico d) South America

22 Cowpea is

a) Day neutral b) Short day

c) Long day d) None of the above

23 Viability of garden pea

a) 4-5 years b) 1 year

c) 6 years d) 2-3 years

24 Goma Manjari is a variety of

a) French bean b) Pea

c) Cluster bean d) Winged bean

25 Botanical name of cowpea

a) *Vicia faba* b) *Vigna unguiculata*

c) *Phaseolus vulgaris* d) *Pisum sativum*

26 Seed rate of broad bean

a) 70-100kg/ha b) 80-110kg/ha

c) 40-50kg/ha d) 30-45kg/ha

27 Yam bean is commercially propagated by

a) Suckers b) Cuttings

c) Seeds d) All of the above

28 Botanical name of jack bean

a) *Glycine soja* b) *Glycine max*

c) *Canavalia gladiate* d) *Canavalia ensiformis*

29 Ancestor of cowpea

a) *Vigna unguilata var. cylindrica* b) *Vigna unguilata var. mensensii*

c) *Vigna unguilata var. radiata* d) *Vigna unguilata var. biflora*

30 Field pea is

a) *Pisum sativum var. arvense* b) *Pisum sativum var. Hortense*

c) *Pisum sativum var. fulvum* d) *Pisum sativum var. humile*

31 Ancestor of pea

a) *Pisum humile* b) *Pisum elatius*

c) *Pisum fulvum* d) *Pisum abyssinicum*

32 Pod maturity of garden pea is determined by

a) Refractometer b) Durometer

c) Tendrometer d) None of the above

33 Inflorescence of French Bean

a) Cymose b) Raceme

c) Both a and b d) None of the above

34 Progenitor of French Bean

a) *Phaseolus lunatas* b) *Phaseolus coccineus*

c) *Phaseolus acutifolius* d) *Phaseolus aborigineus*

35 Rewa variety of Indian Bean protein content

a) 25.11 b) 30.23

b) 40.23 d) 22.12

36 Pusa Parvati is a mutant of

a) Arka Anoop b) Wax pod

c) Arka bold d) Arka komal

37 At what moisture content percentage seeds are extracted and dried?

a) 8-9 % b) 7-8 %

c) 10-12 % d) 5-6 %

38 Pusa Phalguni is introduced from

a) Mexico b) America

c) Philippines d) Africa

39 Pusa Sumeet is a variety of

a) Pea b) French Bean

c) Cowpea d) Broad Bean

40 Vegetable of 20th century is

a) Yam Bean b) Winged Bean

c) Pea d) French Bean

41 Winged Bean tuber contains protein

a) 9-8% b) 12-15%

c) 13-15% d) 10-12%

42 Sowing time of Pea in North Indian Plains

a) October-Mid November b) March-April

c) June-July d) December

43 How much is the isolation distance between two varieties in French bean?

a) 50 m and 40 m b) 30 m and 20 m

c) 60 m and 50 m d) 40 m and 25 m

44 When pods are harvested in French bean?

a) Yellow stage b) Brown stage

c) Full- ripe stage d) Half-ripe stage

45 How is seed extracted in garden pea?

a) Threshing. b) Winnowing

c) Manually d) None of the above

46 What is the safe moisture percentage for storage of garden pea?

a) 7% b) 5 %

c) 9% d) 8 %

47 Bonneville variety is Introduced from

a) Mexico b) Sweden

c) Africa d) USA

48 Highest productivity of Pea is in

a) Karnataka b) Andhra Pradesh

c) Jammu and Kashmir d) Punjab

49 Optimum temperature for growth and yield of French bean is

a) 10-18°C b) 20-25°C

c) 26-27°C d) 22-26°C

50 Sowing time of French bean in hills

a) April-June b) May-June

c) Sept-Nov d) Dec-Jan

51 Dancing style of stigma is present in

a) Broad Bean b) Cowpea

c) Pea d) Bean

52 Rajendra Mishri Kant is a variety of

a) Jack bean b) French Bean

c) Cluster bean d) Yam bean

53 Arkel variety is introduced from

a) Sweden b) America

c) England d) USA

54 Smooth seeded variety is

a) Bonneville b) Meteor

c) Early Badger d) Arkel

55 Yam bean seed oil percentage

a) 20-28% b) 30-40%

b) 29-30% d) 19-20%

56 Gotani bean is

a) *Canavalia gladiate* b) *Glycine max*

b) *Pachyrrhizus erosus* d) *Canavalia plagosperma*

57 Origin of winged bean

a) USA b) Madagascar

c) Mexico d) Africa

58 Broad bean is also known as

a) Faba bean b) Horse bean

c) Bakla bean d) All of the above

59 Yam bean is

a) Long day b) Day neutral

c) Short day d) None of the above

60 Botanical name of Yam bean

a) *Pachyrrhizus erosus* b) *Vicia faba*

c) *Phaseolus vulgaris* d) None of the above

61 Chromosome number of Broad Bean

a) 10 b) 12

c) 18 d) 16

62 Botanical name of Lima Bean

a) *Phaseolus polyanthus* b) *Phaseolus aborigineus*

c) *Phaseolus filiformis* d) *Phaseolus lunatus*

63 Pea is a self-pollinated crop due to presence of

a) Cleistogamous flower b) Chasmogamous flower

c) Both a and b d) None of the above

64 All plant parts are edible in

a) Pea b) Cowpea

c) Winged bean d) Cluster bean

65 Pusa Parvati is resistant to

a) Mosaic b) Powdery mildew

c) Both a and b d) None of the above

66 Iilness to human is caused due to allergy of pollen and green pod of broad bean which is known as

a) Botulism b) Hay fever

c) Asthama d) Favism

67 Velvet Bean is

a) *Glycine max* b) *Mucuma deeringiana*

c) *Phaseolus lunatus* d) *Pachyrrhizus erosus*

68 The colour of the Breeder seed Tag is of

a) Golden Yellow b) Off White

c) Azure Blue d) Bottle Green

69 Careful and systematic evaluation of a seed production field and the removal of all undesirable plants of the same crop is known as

a) Weeding b) Rouging

c) Off-type removal d) Cropping

70 The seed rules were passed in the year

a) 1963 b) 1966

c) 1968 d) 1971

71 Most common breeding procedure used for improvement in French bean

a) Mass selection b) Pureline method

c) Recurrent selection d) Pedigree method

72 Pod colour in French bean is controlled by a single recessive gene

a) a b) z

c) s d) y

73 Botanical name of cluster bean is

a) *Cyamopsis senegalensis* b) *Pisum sativum*

c) *Vigna unguiculata* d) *Cyamopsis tetragonolobus*

74 Pusa Udit is a variety of

a) Broad bean b) Pea

c) Indian bean d) Cluster bean

75 Toxic substance present in young plants of cluster bean

a) Phenol b) Hydrocyanic acid

c) Florigen d) HCL

76 Tender crop and cascade cultivars of French bean is suitable

a) Table purpose b) Canning

c) Processing d) None of the above

77 Transverse cotyledon cracking is a major physiology disorder in

a) Lablab bean b) Pea

c) Yam bean d) French bean

78 Andean yam bean is

a) *Pachyrrhizus tuberosus* b) *Pachyrrhizus erosus*

c) *Pachyrrhizus ahipa* d) None of the above

79 Arka Ajit is resistant to

a) Powdery mildew b) Rust

c) Both a and b d) All of the above

80 Most popular variety of Madhya Pradesh

a) Arkel b) Meteor

c) Asauiji d) Khaper Kheda

81 African yam bean is

a) *Sphentylis stenocarpa* b) *Canavalia gladiate*

c) *Pisum sativum* d) None of the above

82 Anthracnose of common bean is caused by

a) MLOs

b) *Colletotrichum lindemuthianum*

c) Virus

d) *Rhizoctonia solani*

83 Pod straightness is important trait in

a) Processing b) Freezing

c) Dehydration d) Canning

84 Catjang bean is

a) *Phaseolus vulgaris* b) *Vigna unguigulats var.biflora*

c) *Vicia faba* d) *Vigna sinensis var.cylindrica*

85 Pole types are generally

a) Photosensitive b) Photoinsensitive

c) Both a and b d) None of the above

86 White seed is preferred by breeders controlled by recessive gene

a) y b) b

b) h d) p

87 Pea variety tolerant to salinity

a) New line perfection b) Market price

c) Duke of Albany d) All of the above

88 Cluster bean contains a mucilaginous substance in seed known as

a) Tannins b) Saponins

c) Galactomannan d) Sucrose

89 Botanical name of cluster bean

a) *Pisum sativum* b) *Cyamposis tetragonolobus*

c) *Phaseolus vulgaris* d) *Vicia faba*

90 Avoiding out crossing by keeping the crop in isolation is a very effective tool to maintain genetic purity of

a) Self pollinated crops b) Cross pollinated crops

c) Vegtatively propagated crops d) Cereals

91 Bacterial wilt is the most serious disease of

a) Cluster bean b) Cowpea

c) Winged bean d) Pea

92 Snap pea is

a) *Pisum sativum* b) *Pisum elatius*

b) *Pisum stivum var. arvense* d) *Pisum sativum var. macrocarpon*

93 Seed yield of garden pea

a) 1500-2000kg/ha b) 3000-3500kg/ha

c) 2000-2500kg/ha d) 5000-6000kg/ha

94 Chromosome number of winged bean

a) 2n=2x=12 b) 2n=2x=19

c) 2n=2x=18 d) 2n=2x=22

95 Germination of pea is

a) Epigeal b) Hypogeal

c) Exogeal d) Epihypogial

96 Pulse type dolichos bean

a) *Dolichos lablab var.typicus* b) *Dolichos lablab var. lignosus*

c) *Lablab purpureus* d) None of the above

97 Which type of root system is found in pea

a) Fibrous root b) Deep root

b) Flat root d) Tap root

98 Pea production out of total vegetable production is

a) 2.40% b) 5.6%

c) 40% d) 80%

99 Cold tolerance species of French bean

a) *P. filiformis* b) *P. polystachyus*

c) *P. tuberosus* d) *P. acutlifolius*

100 flower color of garden pea

a) Yellow b) Blue

c) Pink d) White

101 Critical stages of irrigation in pea

a) Flower initiation & pod filling stage b) Vegetative stage

c) Ripening stage d) Zigzag stage

102 Hypocotyl cracking is due to low content of

a) Nitrogen b) Calcium

c) Boron d) Zinc

103 Pea is known as

a) Minister of pulses b) Queen of pulses

c) King of pulses d) Dancing star of pulses

104 Single stem variety of cluster bean

a) Pusa Mausami b) Pusa Sadabahar

c) Pusa Navbahar d) Goma Manjiri

105 Training and Stalking is an important intercultural operation in

a) Short varieties of pea plant b) All varieties of pea plant

c) Tall varieties of pea plant d) Nothing such required

106 Moisture required for storage of pea seeds

a) 40-60% b) 100-200%

c) 8-10% d) 20-30%

107 Jacatube bean is

a) *Pachyrrhizus tuberosus* b) *Glycine max*

c) *Pachyrrhizus ahipa* d) None of the above

108 Field pea seeds are

a) Smaller than garden pea seeds b) Larger than garden pea seeds

c) Same like garden pea seeds d) Larger than sugarcane setts

109 Princess Pea is synonym of

a) Cowpea
b) Pea
c) French Bean
d) Winged bean

110 Flower color of field peas

a) Yellow
b) Orange
c) Purple
d) White

111 Black eyed pea is a synonym of

a) Yam Bean
b) Cowpea
c) Pea
d) French Bean

112 Soybeans cannot be eaten raw because of presence of

a) Trypsin inhibitor
b) Niacin inhibitor
c) Iron
d) Pectin

113 What does trypsin do?

a) Mediates the production of ATP
b) Binds with haemoglobin
c) Important for breakdown of proteins
d) Activates hormones

114 The legume is native to India, can tolerate drought and has been cultivated for 3000yrs. This legume is

a) *Vicia faba*
b) *Pisum sativum*
c) None
d) *Arachis hypogea*

115 Which of the following legume was used by Mendel?

a) Broad bean
b) Pea
c) Indian bean
d) French bean

116 Rhizobium and other nitrogen fixing bacteria can reduce atmospheric nitrogen to

a) Ammonia
b) Ammonium
c) Nitrate
d) Nitrite

117 Nodules Are Present On The Roots Of Plants Belonging To The Family?

a) Fabaceae
b) Poaceae
c) Solanaceae
d) Rosaceae

118 Lima bean is useful for

a) Liver
b) Lungs
c) skin
d) All of the above

119 Soybean is an excellent remedy for

a) Childhood malnourishment
b) Skin
c) Both
d) None

120 Legumes have been industrially use to prepare biodegradable plastic, oil, gums, dyes

a) Biodegradable plastic
b) Gums, dyes
c) Oil
d) *All of the above*

121 Which of the following is used as a biofertilizer for soybean crop?

a) Nostoc
b) *Azospirullum*
c) Rhizobium
d) *Anabena*

122 Pick the correct statement

a) legumes do not fix nitrogen
b) legumes fix nitrogen independent of bacteria
c) legumes fix nitrogen through bacteria in their roots
d) legumes fix nitrogen through bacteria in their leaves

123 Protein content in dried French bean seeds (%)

a) 18
b) 25
c) 24
d) 23

124 Recommended seed rate for French bean is _____kg/ha

a) 120
b) 160
c) 130
d) 140

125 Fertilizer recommendation for French bean is _____kg/ha NPK

a) 100:60:20
b) 100:20:0
c) 150:50:50
d) None

126 Beans are affected by which virus

a) BCMV
b) BCMNV
c) Both
d) None

Answer Key

1	a	2	b	3	c	4	d	5	b	6	a	7	c
8	b	9	d	10	a	11	c	12	d	13	a	14	d
15	b	16	c	17	a	18	d	19	b	20	c	21	b
22	a	23	d	24	c	25	b	26	a	27	c	28	d
29	b	30	a	31	b	32	c	33	b	34	d	35	a
36	b	37	a	38	c	39	d	40	b	41	b	42	a
43	a	44	d	45	a	46	c	47	d	48	c	49	b
50	a	51	a	52	d	53	c	54	b	55	a	56	d
57	b	58	d	59	c	60	a	61	b	62	d	63	a
64	c	65	c	66	d	67	b	68	a	69	b	70	c
71	b	72	d	73	d	74	a	75	b	76	c	77	b
78	c	79	c	80	d	81	a	82	b	83	a	84	d
85	a	86	d	87	a	88	c	89	b	90	b	91	a
92	d	93	a	94	c	95	b	96	c	97	d	98	a
99	a	100	d	101	a	102	b	103	b	104	c	105	c
106	c	107	a	108	a	109	d	110	c	111	b	112	a
113	c	114	d	115	b	116	b	117	a	118	d	119	a
120	d	121	c	122	c	123	d	124	a	125	a	126	a

8

Breeding of Vegetable Crops

1 Quantitative characters are governed by

a) Monogene
b) Bi-gene
c) Recessive gene
d) Polygene

2 Monohybrids are derived by hybridizing two individuals which differ for

a) Single-character
b) Double character
c) Quadruple character
d) Multiple character

3 Which phenotypic ratio is expected in F2 in case of complementary gene action

a) 12:3:1
b) 13:3
c) 15:1
d) 9:7

4 Which is a pre-requisite for genetic improvement of vegetable crop

a) Male sterility
b) Genetic variation
c) Sexual reproduction
d) Apomixis

5 Selection provides an opportunity to isolate the promising genotypes from

a) Homogeneous Population
b) Homozygous Population
c) Heterogenous Population
d) Heterozygous Population

6 Homozygosity and homogeneity is maximum in

a) Pure line
b) Inbred line
c) Landraces
d) Synthetic variation

7 Restriction Fragment Length Polymorphism (RFLP) is a

a) Marker Technique
b) Selection method
c) Mutation Technique
d) Gene slicing Technique

8 Which of the following variety in chilli is a result of hybridization

a) G1 b) G2

c) G3 d) G5

9 Heterosis can be fully exploited in

a) Composites b) Hybrids

c) Multilines d) Synthetics

10 To breed for disease resistance which method is used

a) Back cross b) Mass selection

c) Pure Line Selection d) All

11 Okra hybrids are very popular as F1, all are resistant to YVMV governed by

a) Single dominant gene b) Single recessive gene

c) Two recessive gene d) All

12 The Hybrid Onion Programme originated in 1925 by

a) T. W. Whitaker b) B. D. Dowker

c) V. Swarup d) H. A. Jones

13 Which phenotypic ratio is expected in F2 of monohybrid cross

a) 1:2:1 b) 1:1:1

c) 3:1 d) 2:1:1

14 How many genotypes will be possible in F2 (3n) in the case of trihybrid cross

a) 16 b) 9

c) 27 d) 81

15 Male sterile line is maintained by

a) Crossing with heterozygous b) Male fertile line

c) Both of the above d) None of the above

16 Heterosis is the result of which type of gene effects

a) Over-dominance b) Dominance

c) Additive d) Epistatic

17 Number of single crosses in full diallel are

a) n (n-1) b) n (n-1)/2

c) 2n (n-1)/2 d) n^2

18 Self- Pollination increases

a) Homozygosity b) Heterozygosity

c) Homogeneity d) Heterogeneity

19 The proportion of additive genetic variance to phenotypic variance is called

a) Heterobeltiosis b) Heritability

c) Dominance relationship d) Linkage relationship

20 Sporophtic self-incompatibility system is present in

a) Cabbage b) Tomato

c) Chilli d) Okra

21 In male sterility pollens are

a) Abortive b) Shrivelled

c) Non-functional d) All of the above

22 Sree Shilpa is the first hybrid of

a) Greater yam b) Elephant Foot yam

c) Lesser yam d) White yam

23 Self-incompatibility is overcome by

a) Bud Pollination b) Surgical Techniques

c) Irradiation d) All of these

24 Type of self-incompatibility observed in cole crops

a) Gametophytic b) Sporophytic

c) Both a&b d) None of these

25 Most important factor in a hybridization programme

a) Choice of parents for hybridization

b) Emasculation

c) Handling of segregating generations

d) Pollination

26 Yellow anther type in case of chilli is

a) Bhagya Lakshmi b) Jwalamukhi

c) Andhra Jyoti d) Bhaskar

27 Male sterility is common in

a) Carrot b) Bean

c) Okra d) None

28 Male sterile line in Onion is isolated from

a) Pusa Red b) Pusa Ratnar

c) Pusa Madhavi d) Arka Bindu

29 In vegetable improvement programmes which is most commonly used

a) Interspecific Hybridization b) Intergeneric Hybridization

c) Intervarietal Hybridization d) Distant Hybridization

30 Jade Cross is a F1 hybrid of

a) Brussels sprout b) Sprouting Brocolli

c) Knol- Khol d) Cabbage

31 The F1 hybrid in the case of Muskmelon is

a) Pusa Madhuras b) Pusa Rasraj

c) Arka Rajhans d) Arka Jeet

32 In Onion ———— is used as a maintainer line for male sterile line

a) Smsms b) Nmsms

c) NMsMs d) NMsms

33 Pusa red Plum variety of Tomato has the highest Vit-C content and is developed through

a) Intervarietal crosses b) Interspecific crosses

c) Intergeneric crosses d) Intraspecific crosses

34 Selfing and Massing technique of breeding (Improvement in a cultivar can be affected by selfing followed by massing) was suggested by

a) Clarke (1943) b) Jones and Mann

c) Pirovano (1972) d) None

35 Pusa Parvati, an improved cultivar of French bean resistant to mosaic and powdery mildew and suitable for hills was developed by

a) Selection b) Hybridization

c) Mutation d) Polyploidy

36 Somatic hybrids of *Solanum melongena and S. sisimbrifolium* was made possible through

a) Embryo rescue b) Protoplast fusion

c) Micropropagation d) Anther culture

37 "Newleaf" is a transgenic of which crop commercialized by Monsanto since 1989

a) Potato carrying 3A gene b) Cabbage carrying 3A gene

c) Tomato carrying 3A gene d) Brinjal carrying 3A gene

38 In Onion, the type of self-sterility is

a) Genetic b) Cytoplasmic-genetic

c) Cytoplasmic d) None

39 Pusa Sanyog is a F1 hybrid of

a) Cucumber b) Muskmelon

c) Watermelon d) Long melon

40 Pinching of male flowers is effective in

a) Bottlegourd b) Cucumber

c) Muskmelon d) Watermelon

41 F1 generation in potato itself produces enough variations due to

a) Heterozygosity of parents b) Auto tetraploidy

c) Both a &b d) None

42 The most widely used male sterility system

a) CMS b) GMS

c) CGMS d) CHA's

43 The method of breeding where the single seed is collected from each plant to grow next generation is

a) Single Plant selection b) Pure line selection

c) Single seed descent d) Mass selection

44 In mutation breeding of self-pollinated crop, a recessive mutation induced by mutagen is detected in

a) M1 generation b) M 2 generation

c) M3 generation d) M4 generation

45 Desirable features of female parent in hybrid seed production of cabbage is

a) Self-incompatible b) Self-compatible

c) Cross compatible d) Both a &c

46 Formation of anther cone surrounding the stigma leading to self-pollination is seen in _______ crop

a) Tomato b) Lettuce

c) Pea d) Brinjal

47 Which of the following is not a breeding method in brinjal

a) Pedigree b) Pure Line selection

c) Bulk method d) Mass selection

48 The parentage of Pusa Sharbati (musk melon) is

a) Kutana x PMR-6 b) Hara Madhu x Edisto

c) MS-1 x Hara Madhu d) M-3 x Durgapur Madhu

49 Genetic purity of seed lot can be determined by

a) Progeny test b) Grow-out test

c) Chi-square test d) T-test

50 Johannsen proposed the pure line theory on the basis of seed size in crop

a) Potato b) Sweet Potato

c) French bean d) Dolichos beans

51 Which of the following tomato species is used as a donor parent for salt tolerance in Tomato breeding

a) *L. pennellii* b) *L. hirsutum*

c) *L. cheesmanii* d) *L. pimpinellifolium*

52 Genetic variation arises over a period of time because of _________ in the pure line

a) Mechanical mixtures b) Out-crossing

c) Mutation d) All of the above

53 Simple recurrent selection is most suitable for characters with

a) High heritability b) Low heritability

c) Moderate heritability d) All of the above

54 Selection might be started from ______ for simply inherited characters

a) F1 b) F2

c) F3 d) F4

55 In which of the following families, Incompatibility is common

a) Malvaceae b) Rosaceae

c) Liliaceae d) Poaceae

56 Severe inbreeding depression is seen in

a) Self-Pollinated crops

b) Apomixis

c) Cross-pollinated crops and vegetatively propagated crops

d) Seed propagated crops

57 A cross between an inbred line and an open-pollinated variety is called

a) Test cross b) Back cross

c) Top cross d) Poly cross

58 Which type of gametes are produced by nullisomic

a) n+1 b) n-1

c) n d) n+1-1

59 Which of the following method is only followed in cross-pollinated crops

a) Back cross method b) Pedigree method

c) Mass selection d) Recurrent selection

60 Production of ——— is done by anther culture

a) Diploid plants b) Polyploid plants

c) Haploid plants d) Triploid plants

61 Which scientist made the first intergeneric cross between radish and cabbage

a) Hull (1945) b) Rimpu (1890)

c) Andrew Knight (1800) d) Karpenchenko (1927)

62 Ty-1 gene conferring resistance to TLVC is derived from

a) *Solanum chilense* b) *Solanum habrochaites*

c) *Solanum torvum* d) *Solanum lycopersicum*

63 The number of linkage groups in Table Beet are

a) 9 b) 18

c) 6 d) 11

64 In recessive epistasis, the phenotypic ratio 9:3:3:1 is modified to

a) 9:3:4 b) 9:7

c) 15:1 d) 12:3:1

65 Male parent for development of chilli hybrid 'CH-3' is

a) LLS b) S-2560

c) S-2530 d) Punjab Lal

66 Mass selection is based on the

a) Progeny test b) Maternal parent only

c) Paternal parent only d) Both parents

67 The genomic constitution of *Brassica carinata is*

a) AABB b) AACC

c) BBCC d) AABBCC

68 Selfing reduces heterozygosity in each generation by the factor

a) 1/4 b) 1/3

c) 1/2 d) 1/8

69 In self-pollinated crops, cross-pollination varies from

a) 5-10% b) 20-30%

c) 30-50% d) 50-70%

70 What is the optimum dose of mutagen for effective treatment

a) LD_{50} b) Close to LD_{50}

c) Lower than LD_{50} d) Higher than LD_{50}

71 Which of the following is PCR based marker

a) SSR b) RFLP

c) RAPD d) Both a & c

72 Male sterility found in Carrot is

a) CMS b) GMS

c) CGMS d) Both a & c

Answer Key

1	d	2	a	3	a	4	b	5	c	6	a	7	a
8	a	9	b	10	a	11	a	12	d	13	c	14	c
15	b	16	b	17	a	18	a	19	b	20	d	21	d
22	b	23	d	24	b	25	a	26	d	27	a	28	a
29	c	30	a	31	c	32	a	33	b	34	b	35	c
36	b	37	a	38	b	39	a	40	a	41	b	42	c
43	c	44	b	45	d	46	a	47	d	48	a	49	b
50	c	51	c	52	d	53	a	54	b	55	b	56	c
57	c	58	b	59	d	60	c	61	b	62	b	63	a
64	a	65	c	66	b	67	c	68	c	69	a	70	a
71	a	72	d										

9

Seed Production of Vegetable Crops

1 What is the isolation distance for raising foundation seed in bottle gourd?

a) 800 m b) 700 m

c) 600 m d) 500 m

2 Roguing of off-type plants in bottle gourd seed production should be done at how many stages?

a) Three b) Four

c) Two d) Five

3 Where are bottle gourd seeds stored after extraction?

a) Open containers b) Shade

c) Air tight containers d) Open

4 What is the isolation distance for raising certified seed in bitter gourd?

a) 300 m b) 200 m

c) 250 m d) 500 m

5 The off-types in bitter gourd should be removed at which stage of rouging?

a) Before flowering b) After flowering

c) Harvesting d) Vegetative stage

6 What should be the colour of bitter gourd fruits at the time of seed harvesting?

a) Brown b) Black

c) Yellowish-orange d) Green

7 Seed yield of bitter gourd is?

a) 100-200 kg/ha b) 400-500 kg/ha

c) 200-300 kg/ha d) 600-700 kg/ha

8 What is the minimum germination percentage for bitter gourd foundation and certified seeds?

a) 60% b) 80%

c) 50% d) 30%

9 What is the Isolation distance for foundation seed in brinjal?

a) 100 m b) 400 m

c) 300 m d) 200 m

10 What is the Isolation distance for certified seed in brinjal?

a) 100 m b) 300 m

c) 100 m d) 200 m

11 What is the isolation distance for certified seed production?

a) 2000 m b) 1000 m

c) 500 m d) 200 m

12 What is the pollination agent of Cauliflower?

a) Bees b) Wasps

c) Ants d) Houseflies

13 Which is the pollination mechanism in Cauliflower?

a) Self-pollination b) Often-cross pollination

c) Cross pollination d) None of the above

14 Which growth regulator used to increase seed quality in Cauliflower?

a) Gibberllins b) Auxin

c) ABA d) Nepthaleneacetic acid (NAA)

15 How many season are required for seed production in cabbage?

a) 4 seasons b) 3 seasons

c) 2 seasons d) 6 seasons

16 Which method of seed production is followed to produce certified seeds?

a) Seed to Seed b) Head to seed

c) Seed to Head d) All of the above

17 Which method of seed production is followed to produce Nuclear seeds?

a) Seed to Head b) Seed only

c) Head to Seed d) None of the above

18 Which is the commonly used treatment for protection against seed borne diseases?

a) Hot water treatment
b) Cold water treatment
c) Physical treatment
d) Chemical treatment

19 What is the required temperature for hot water treatment?

a) 30°C
b) 50°C
c) 45°C
d) 40°C

20 Which is the recommended method for seed production of kale?

a) Furrow method
b) Dibbling
c) Broadcasting
d) Replanting method

21 What is the isolation distance for production of foundation seeds in Kale?

a) 400 m
b) 200 m
c) 1000 m
d) 500 m

22 What is the spacing kept in kale for seed production?

a) 30 x 45 cm
b) 20 x 45 cm
c) 30 x 40 cm
d) 40 x 45 cm

23 What should be the moisture per cent in dried seeds of kale?

a) 8%
b) 10%
c) 7%
d) 12%

24 What is the best seed extraction methods in tomato?

a) Alkali method
b) Fermentation method
c) Acid method
d) None of above

25 Moisture percentfor safe storage in tomato

a) 8-9 %
b) 10-12 %
c) 12-13 %
d) 6-7 %

26 What is the isolation distance for certified seed production of chilli?

a) 400 m
b) 600 m
c) 300 m
d) 500 m

27 Chilli is

a) Self-pollinated
b) Cross-pollinated
c) Often cross-pollinated crop
d) None of the above

28 At what stage is chilli harvested for seed purposes?

a) Fully ripe stage
b) Half ripe stage
c) Green stage
d) None of the above

29 What type of pollination is found in Lettuce?

a) Cross-pollination
b) Often-cross pollination
c) Self-pollination
c) All of the above

30 What type of flowers Carrot have?

a) Gynoecious
b) Pistillate
c) Protandrous
d) Staminate

31 What is the ideal spacing between the rows and plants for onion seed production?

a) 40 cm x 10 cm
b) 30 cm x 10 cm
c) 30 cm x 20 cm
d) 30 cm x 40 cm

32 How much is the isolation distance for foundation and certified seed production in brinjal?

a) 200 m, and 100 m
b) 300 m and 400 m
c) 500 m and 1000 m
d) 100 m and 50 m

33 Which are the critical stages for roughing (off-types and diseased plants) brinjal?

a) Pre-flowering
b) Flowering
c) Maturity stage
d) All of the above

34 How much isolation distance is maintained between two varieties for production of foundation and certified seed in sweet and hot chillies?

a) 1000 m and 500 m
b) 500 m and 250 m
c) 400 m and 200 m
d) 200 m and 100 m

35 Which are the critical stages for the removal of off-types, diseased and deformed plants in sweet and hot chillies?

a) Pre-flowering
b) Flowering
b) Fruit maturity
d) All of the above

36 What is the recommended spacing in sweet pepper for seed production?

a) 20 x 20 cm
b) 30 x 30 cm
c) 50 x 60 cm
d) 60 x 60 cm

37 At what moisture content percentage seeds are extracted and dried?

a) 8-9 %
b) 7-8 %
c) 10-12 %
d) 5-6 %

38 What is the isolation distance between two varieties for producing foundation and certified seed in tomato?

a) 30 m and 25 m
b) 60 m and 35 m
c) 45 m and 20 m
d) 50 m and 25 m

39 How many times fields are inspected for seed production in tomato?

a) 4
b) 5
c) 6
d) 2

40 Which chemical to spray for production of hybrid seed in cucumber?

a) ABA
b) Silver nitrate
c) Ethereal
d) Gibberlins

41 At what stage ethereal is sprayed in cucumber for seed production?

a) 2 and 4 leaf stage.
b) 3 and 4 leaf stage
c) 5 and 6 leaf stage
d) 4 and 5 leaf stage

42 How much is the isolation distance between two varieties for raising foundation and certified seed in cucurbits?

a) 500 m and 200 m
b) 800 m and 500 m
c) 100m and 200 m
d) 700 m and 400 m

43 How much is the isolation distance between two varieties in French bean?

a) 50 m and 40 m
b) 30 m and 20 m
c) 60 m and 50 m
d) 40 m and 25 m

44 When pods are harvested in French bean?

a) Yellow stage
b) Brown stage
c) Full- ripe stage
d) Half-ripe stage

45 How is seed extracted in garden pea?

a) Threshing.
b) Winnowing
c) Manually
d) None of the above

46 What is the safe moisture percentage for storage of garden pea?

a) 7%
b) 5 %
c) 9%
d) 8 %

47 How is seed production of cole crops done?

a) Dibbling b) Drilling

c) Harvesting d) Replanting method

48 How much is the isolation distance between two varieties for raising foundation and certified seed in cole crops?

a) 1000 m b) 500 m

c) 600 m d) 400 m

49 How much is the isolation distance between two varieties for raising foundation and certified seed in carrots?

a) 800 m and 400 m b) 400 m and 200 m

c) 1000 and 800 m d) 500 m and 250 m

50 How much is the isolation distance for foundation and certified seed in radish?

a) 1500 and 1000 m b) 1000 m and 1500m

c) 1000 m and 500 m d) 500 m and 400 m

51 What is the spacing for seed production in Onion?

a) 50 x 20 cm. b) 40 x 20 cm.

c) 60 x 20 cm. d) 80 x 20 cm

52 How much is the recommended spacing for seed production in sweet pepper?

a) 40 x 40 cm b) 60 x 60 cm

c) 50 x 50 cm d) 20 x 20 cm

53 How to increase seed yield in cucurbits?

a) Hand pollination b) Self-pollination

c) Cross-pollination d) None of the above

54 What is the recommended spacing for seed production in cabbage?

a) 35 x 70cm. b) 55 x 60cm.

c) 45 x 60cm. d) 45 x 70cm.

55 What is the recommended spacing for seed production in knolkhol?

a) 30 x 45cm b) 20 x 45cm

b) 60 x 45cm d) 50 x 45cm

56 What is the recommended spacing for seed production in kale?

a) 20 x 45 cm b) 60 x 45 cm

b) 30 x 45 cm d) 50 x 45 cm

57 How much FYM is applied during seed production of cole crops?

a) 35 – 40 t/ha. b) 45 – 60 t/ha.

c) 25 – 30 t/ha. d) 55 – 80 t/ha.

58 How much N is applied for seed production of cole crops?

a) 80 kg/ha b) 70 kg/ha

c) 50 kg/ha d) 90 kg/ha

59 How much P is applied during cole crops seed production?

a) 70 kg/ha b) 90 kg/ha

c) 100 kg/ha d) 60 kg/ha

60 How much K is applied during seed production of cole crops?

a) 80 kg/ha b) 90 kg/ha

c) 100 kg/ha d) 70 kg/ha

61 How much is the spacing for raising seed crop in carrot?

a) 60 cm x 30 cm b) 70 cm x 20 cm

c) 80 cm x 30 cm d) 50 cm x 10 cm

62 How much is the spacing for raising seed crop in radish?

a) 70 cm x 30 cm b) 80 cm x 30 cm

c) 90 cm x 30 cm d) 60 cm x 30 cm

63 How much is the spacing for raising seed crop in turnip?

a) 60 cm x 30 cm b) 90 cm x 30 cm

c) 100 cm x 30 cm d) 50 cm x 30 cm

64 How much is the safe moisture percentage in root crops?

a) 10-12% b) 9-10 %

c) 12-15 % d) 11-13 %

65 What is the isolation distance between onion varieties?

a) 400m b) 500m

c) 1500m d) 1000m

66 The head quarter of PPV&FR is located at

a) Hyderabad b) Bangaluru

c) Lucknow d) New Delhi

67 The colour of the tag of Foundation seed I is of

a) Golden Yellow b) White

c) Azure Blue d) Bottle Green

68 The colour of the Breeder seed Tag is of

a) Golden Yellow b) Off White

c) Azure Blue d) Bottle Green

69 Careful and systematic evaluation of a seed production field and the removal of all undesirable plants of the same crop is known as

a) Weeding b) Rouging

c) Off-type removal d) Cropping

70 The seed rules were passed in the year

a) 1963 b) 1966

c) 1968 d) 1971

71 Minimum gap required for seed production programme of different varieties of the same vegetable crop in the selected field is

a) 1-2 year b) 2-3 years

c) 3-4 years d) 4-5 year

72 Seed production plot should be under

a) Sole cropping b) Inter cropping

c) Mixed cropping d) None of the above

73 Plants formed by the seed of the crop grown last year in the same field is known as

a) Off type b) Rogue

c) Volunteer plant d) Objectionable weed

74 At head formation stage a cross shape cut is made for seed stalk emergence in

a) Egyptian clover b) Potato

c) Cabbage d) Castor

75 To induce seed stalk formation horizontal cut is made on the

a) Curd of cauliflower b) Sugarcane sett

c) Potato tuber d) Sweet potato

76 Seed rate of true potato seed for one hectare is

a) 2.5t/ha b) 1kg/ha

c) 100 kg/ha d) 100g/ha

77 Nucleus seed of carrot is produced by

a) Seed to seed method b) Seed to root method

c) Root to seed method d) Any method

78 Minimum number of seeds tested for germination is

a) 200 b) 400

c) 500 d) 100

79 The purity of the seed that is improved by rouging is

a) Physical purity b) Geneticpurity

c) Ethic purity d) Expressedpurity

80 Seed plot is grown at a particular distance from the sources of genetic contamination to avoid

a) Self -pollination b) Out crossing

c) Gaitenogamy d) Crosspollination

81 The pollen grains are tested for viability by using solution

a) Carmine b) Iodine solution

c) Agar agar d) Commusiveblue

82 Foundation seed producer transfers the seed to

a) Seed Corporation b) Seed Processing Plant

c) Seed Certification Agency d) The University

83 Among the following crops the highest physical purity percentage for seed certification is required for

a) Wheat b) Rice

c) Cabbage d) Okra

84 The highest seed replacement rate is of

a) A Synthetic b) A Composite

c) A hybrid d) A variety

85 Rouging is a very effective tool to maintain genetic purity of

a) Self pollinated crops

b) Cross pollinated crops

c) Often cross pollinated crops

d) Vegetatively propagated crops

86 Tetrazoluim test was evolved by

a) G. Lakon b) M. Mchargue

b) G. Gadd d) A. Eidmann

87 The father of seed technology is

a) M. Mchargue b) Gadd

c) C. Eidmann d) Friedrich Nobbe

88 Male Sterile Hybrid is formed in

a) CMS b) GMS

c) CGMS d) CHA

89 Selection involved in maintenance breeding is

a) Negative b) Positive

c) Neutral d) Recurrent

90 Avoiding out crossing by keeping the crop in isolation is a very effective tool to maintain genetic purity of

a) Self pollinated crops b) Cross pollinated crops

c) Vegtatively propagated crops d) Cereals

91 An isolation distance is maintained between two

a) Genera

b) Crops

c) Cross incompatible species of the same genera

d) Varieties of the same crop

92 The field infected by brown rot, wart or nematode should not be selected for seed production of

a) Potato tubers b) Sugarcane

b) Onion d) Soybean

93 True seed of potato is formed in

a) Pod b) Tuber

c) Micro-tuber d) Berry

94 Diaphanoscope is used to test the

a) Physical purity b) Genetic purity

c) Moisture content d) Moisture content

95 For production of foundation seed, the sowing will be of class seed.

a) Nucleus seed b) Breeder seed

c) Foundation seed d) Certified seed

96 Seeds Control Order under the Essential Commodities Act, 1955 was enacted in the year

a) 1981 b) 1983

c) 1987 d) 1988

97 National Seed Policy was enacted in the year

a) 1966 b) 1968

b) 1998 d) 2002

98 Plant of same variety with different expression mainly for phenological traits is removed form the seed production plot to reduce

a) Genetic shift b) Genetic drift

c) Genetic erosion d) Genetic identity

99 Certification of seed is done at

a) One level b) Two levels

c) Three levels d) Four levels

100 New Policy on Seed Development was enacted in the year

a) 1988 b) 1985

c) 1998 d) 2008

Answer Key

1	a	2	b	3	c	4	d	5	a	6	c	7	c
8	a	9	d	10	a	11	b	12	a	13	c	14	d
15	c	16	a	17	c	18	a	19	b	20	d	21	c
22	a	23	c	24	a	25	b	26	a	27	c	28	a
29	c	30	c	31	b	32	a	33	a	34	c	35	a
36	d	37	a	38	d	39	a	40	c	41	a	42	b
43	a	44	d	45	a	46	c	47	d	48	a	49	c
50	a	51	c	52	b	53	a	54	c	55	a	56	b
57	c	58	d	59	b	60	a	61	a	62	d	63	a
64	c	65	d	66	d	67	b	68	a	69	b	70	b
71	a	72	a	73	c	74	c	75	a	76	d	77	c
78	c	79	b	80	b	81	a	82	b	83	d	84	c
85	a	86	a	87	d	88	a	89	b	90	a	91	b
92	a	93	d	94	a	95	b	96	d	97	d	98	b
99	b	100	a										

10

Organic Farming

1. Who is often referred to as the father of organic farming?

   a) J.I. Rodale
   b) Sir Albert Howard
   c) Rudolf Steiner
   d) Rachel Carson

2. Which organization is responsible for setting and regulating organic farming standards in the United States?

   a) United Nations (UN)
   b) World Health Organization (WHO)
   c) United States Department of Agriculture (USDa)
   d) Environmental Protection Agency (EPA)

3. What is the main purpose of organic farming standards and regulations?

   a) To promote the use of synthetic pesticides
   b) To ensure the production of genetically modified organisms (GMOs)
   c) To establish guidelines for sustainable and environmentally friendly farming practices
   d) To encourage monoculture farming

4. What does the term "certified organic" mean?

   a) It ensures that products meet specific organic farming standards and have been inspected by certifying bodies
   b) It indicates that the product is genetically modified.
   c) It guarantees the absence of all pesticides in organic products
   d) It denotes that the product is not suitable for human consumption.

5. Which label is used for products that meet both organic and fair trade standards, emphasizing ethical and sustainable production?

   a) "Certified Sustainable"
   b) "Fair and Organic"
   c) " Organic Fair Trade"
   d) "Ethical Organic"

6 What is the role of certification bodies in the context of organic farming standards?

a) They are responsible for setting the standards

b) They inspect and certify that farms and products meet organic standards

c) They promote the use of synthetic pesticides in organic farming

d) They handle marketing and distribution of organic products.

7 Which component of organic farming standards ensures transparency and traceability in the organic supply chain?

a) Organic certification

b) Pest management

c) Crop diversity

d) Soil health

8 What is one of the key factors that can make organic farming more economically challenging compared to conventional farming?

a) Higher demand for synthetic pesticides

b) Government subsidies for organic farmers

c) Lower crop yields

d) Reduced labor costs

9 In organic farming, what is a common reason for the higher market price of organic products?

a) Lower production costs

b) Increased pesticide use

c) Growing only one type of crop

d) Premium prices due to consumer demand

10 Which method of organic farming relies on the natural interactions between different species to control pests and enhance crop growth?

a) Crop rotation

b) Synthetic pesticides

c) Polyculture

d) Monoculture

11 What is the primary purpose of cover cropping in organic farming?

a) To increase monoculture practices

b) To enhance soil fertility and prevent erosion

c) To control pests using synthetic chemicals

d) To eliminate crop diversity

12 Which practice involves using beneficial insects to control harmful pests in organic farming?

a) Synthetic pesticide application b) Crop rotation

c) Biological pest control d) Monoculture

13 What is the purpose of composting in organic farming?

a) To dispose of organic waste

b) To create synthetic fertilizers

c) To convert organic matter into nutrient-rich soil amendments

d) To eradicate all soil microorganisms

14 Which method aims to reduce soil erosion and enhance soil structure in organic farming?

a) Synthetic pesticide application b) No-till farming

c) Monoculture d) Overgrazing

15 Which practice involves using manure and compost as sources of nutrients in organic farming?

a) Synthetic fertilizer application

b) Organic nutrient management

c) Monoculture

d) Crop rotation

16 Which aspect of organic farming standards focuses on the avoidance of synthetic chemicals and genetically modified organisms (GMOs)?

a) Soil health b) Pest management

c) Prohibited substances d) Crop diversity

17 What is the primary goal of organic livestock standards?

a) To encourage crowded and unsanitary animal living conditions

b) To promote the use of synthetic growth hormones and antibiotics

c) To ensure the well-being of animals and their access to organic feed

d) To maximize meat production regardless of animal welfare

18 In organic farming, what is the maximum allowable percentage of non-organic ingredients in processed organic products?

a) 0% b) 25%

c) 50% d) 75%

19 Which of the following is a potential benefit of organic farming for farmers in the long run?

a) Immediate higher profits

b) Lower startup costs

c) Improved soil health and reduced dependence on external inputs

d) Reduced labor requirements

20 Why might organic farmers face higher initial costs compared to conventional farmers?

a) Lower cost of organic certification

b) Reduced need for equipment and infrastructure

c) Investment in organic soil improvement practices

d) Government subsidies for organic farmers

21 In organic farming, what is the potential economic advantage of diversifying crops or adopting crop rotation?

a) Reduced income from the same crop

b) Higher dependence on synthetic fertilizers

c) Lower pest management costs

d) Minimal impact on soil health

22 What role do government subsidies often play in the economics of organic farming?

a) They encourage the use of synthetic pesticides in organic farming

b) They provide financial incentives for farmers to transition to organic practices.

c) They make organic products less expensive for consumers

d) They are not applicable to organic farming.

23 Which factor has a significant influence on the profitability of organic farming?

a) Soil type

b) Government regulations

c) Access to synthetic fertilizers

d) Consumer demand and market prices

24 What is one of the primary challenges associated with organic farming compared to conventional farming?

a) Higher crop yields

b) Increased use of synthetic pesticides

c) Limited pest and disease control options

d) Reduced consumer demand

25 Organic farming often involves the use of natural alternatives for pest control. What is an example of such a method?

a) Frequent synthetic pesticide application

b) Monoculture farming

c) Heavy use of synthetic fertilizers

d) Crop rotation

26 What issue might organic farmers face when trying to source organic seeds for their crops?

a) It is a simple and low-cost process

b) It requires minimal documentation.

c) Small-scale farmers are exempt from certification

b) The costs and paperwork involved can be burdensome.

27 Organic farming typically emphasizes soil health. What issue is associated with this focus on soil quality?

a) Longer-lasting soil fertility

b) Improved water conservation

c) Potentially slower initial crop growth

d) Higher crop yields

28 What can make the transportation and distribution of organic products more challenging than conventional products?

a) Lower demand for organic products

b) Heavier use of preservatives in organic foods

c) Reduced shelf life of organic products

d) need for separate handling and labeling

29 Which region of the world has shown significant growth in organic farming in recent years?

a) North America

b) Antarctica

c) Sub-Saharan Africa

d) Asia

30 Which country is known for being a global leader in organic agriculture and the largest producer of organic foods?

a) China

b) India

c) Brazil

d) Germany

31 What global trend has contributed to the growth of the organic food market?

a) Decreased interest in sustainable agriculture

b) Lower consumer demand for organic products

c) Increased awareness of health and environmental concerns

d) Reduced focus on food quality

32 Which organization serves as the international body for setting organic farming standards and guidelines?

a) International Monetary Fund (IMF)

b) Food and Agriculture Organization (FAO)

c) World Health Organization (WHO)

c) International Federation of Organic Agriculture Movements (IFOAM)

33 In which region are organic farming practices often adopted to combat desertification and improve land sustainability?

a) Europe b) North America

c) Middle East d) South Asia

34 What is the major challenge faced by many developing countries in promoting organic farming

a) High consumer demand for organic products

b) Government subsidies for synthetic pesticides

c) Lack of access to modern agricultural technologies

d) Abundant fertile land

35 Which country has made significant strides in promoting organic farming practices through government policies and incentives?

a) United States b) Australia

c) China d) Japan

36 What is the role of international organic trade agreements and standards?

a) They aim to restrict the global organic trade

b) They limit organic farming to a specific region.

c) They prioritize the use of synthetic pesticides in organic agriculture

d) They harmonize organic standards and facilitate global organic trade.

37 What is the primary government agency responsible for regulating and promoting organic farming in India?

a) Ministry of Health and Family Welfare

b) Ministry of Agriculture and Farmers Welfare

c) Ministry of Environment, Forest and Climate Change

d) Ministry of Commerce and Industry

38 Which state in India is known for being a pioneer in organic farming and is often referred to as the "Organic State"?

a) Maharashtra b) Tamil Nadu

c) Sikkim d) Uttar Pradesh

39 What is the certification mark issued by the Agricultural and Processed Food Products Export Development Authority (APEDA) for organic products in India?

a) NPOP b) FSSAI

c) AGMARK d) BIS

40 Which international organization plays a crucial role in accrediting certification bodies for organic products in India?

a) FAO b) IFOAM

c) ISO d) CITES

41 What percentage of the total organic farming land in India is under the National Program for Organic Production (NPOP) as of 2021?

a) Less than 5% b) Around 20%

c) Approximately 50% d) Over 80%

42 What is the role of the Participatory Guarantee System (PGS) in organic farming in India?

a) It provides organic certification for exports

b) It regulates pesticide use in organic farming.

c) It offers a certification process tailored for small-scale organic farmers

d) It manages international organic trade agreements.

43 When did the modern organic farming movement begin?

a) 18th century b) 19th century

c) 21st century d) 20th century

44 Which agricultural method influenced the development of organic farming principles in the early 20th century?

a) Industrial agriculture
b) Biodynamic farming
c) Green Revolution
d) Hydroponics

45 The term "organic farming" was first coined in which decade?

a) 1990s
b) 1970s
c) 1930s
d) 1950s

46 Which book by Sir Albert Howard played a pivotal role in the organic farming movement?

a) "The Omnivore's Dilemma"
b) "An Agricultural Testament"
c) "The Silent Spring"
d) "Our Stolen Future"

47 What key principle distinguishes organic farming from conventional farming?

a) Irrigation methods
b) Crop rotation
c) Synthetic pesticide use
d) Mechanized equipment

48 What is the primary goal of organic pest management?

a) Eliminating all pests using chemical pesticides
b) Maintaining a pest-free environment
c) Balancing pest populations through natural methods
d) Encouraging the use of synthetic fertilizers

49 What is the primary objective of organic weed management?

a) Eliminating all weeds using chemical herbicides
b) Promoting weed growth for increased biodiversity
c) Controlling weeds using natural methods
d) Encouraging monoculture practices

50 What is the role of mulching in organic farming?

a) To eliminate all insects and pests
b) To protect the soil, conserve moisture, and control weeds
c) To maximize synthetic fertilizer application
d) To promote monoculture practices

51 Which type of process composting is?

a) Self heating
b) Aerobic biological
c) Thermophilic
d) All of the above

52 The cow dung + urine + agricultural waste are ready to be used as farm yard manure after how many days?

a) 30 – 50 days
b) 50 – 90 days
c) 90 to 120 days
d) 120 to 150 days

53 What is the percent amount of nitrogen, phosphorus, and potash in farm yard manure?

a) 0.5, 0.2, and 0.3
b) 0.3, 0.5, and 0.2
c) 0.7, 0.5, and 0.3
d) None of the above.

54 Which is a bulky organic manure?

a) Farm Yard Manure
b) Green manure
c) Oil cakes
d) All of the above

55 _________ is a microbial pesticide

a) Bacillus thuringiensis
b) Trichograma
c) Both a and b
d) None of the above

56 How would you limit nutrient loss?

a) Proper recycling of wastes
b) Synchronizing release and uptake of nutrients
c) Proper handling of organic wastes
d) All of the above

57 Which is not a component of Organic Farming?

a) Non-chemical weed control measures
b) Biological pest management
c) Farm Yard Manure
d) Synthetic pesticides

58 Which is true about Organic Farming?

a) We have to feed crop
b) We have to feed soil
c) Both a and b
d) None of the above

59 What is the full form of IFOAM?

a) International Federation of Organic Agriculture Movements

b) Indian Federation of Organic Agriculture Movements

c) Italian Federation of Organic Agriculture Movements

d) Industrial Federation of Organic Agriculture movements

60 In which year IFOAM was established?

a) 1970 b) 1972

c) 1971 d) 1973

61 In organic farming, what is the primary source of soil fertility and nutrients for vegetables?

a) Synthetic chemical fertilizers

b) Organic compost, manure, and cover crops

c) Herbicides

d) Hydroponics

62 Which country represents the lowest percentage of area under organic farming out of the cultivated area?

a) India b) Australia

c) China d) USA

63 What is a major component of the organic farming/cultivation system ?

a) Pesticides b) Synthetic fertilizers

c) Chemical fertilizers d) Bio Fertilzers

64 Growing green manure crops in the field and incorporating in its green stage in the same field is known ?

a) Ex situ green manuring b) In situ green manuring

c) Green leaf manuring d) None of the above

65 The breeding and rearing of earthworms in a controlled environment is called ?

a) Vermiwash b) Vermiculture

c) Vermicomposting d) Vermicasting

66 Azolla Biofertilizer is mainly used in which of the following crop ?

a) Jowar b) Rice/Paddy

c) Maize d) Millets

67 The main organic product export market for india is?

a) China b) USA

c) Canada d) Europe

68 Which of these is not allowed in organic cultivation?

a) Sewage sludge b) Crop rotation

c) Cover crops a) Buffer zones

69 Which is the main source of water for organic cultivation in India ?

a) Rivers b) Oceans

c) Tanks d) Wells/Borewells

70 The best practice to maintain soil health in organic farming is

a) Crop rotation b) Synthetic fertilizers

c) Using black soil d) Monoculture

71 How many years the land/soil must be treated as organic without using any prohibited chemicals and other substances to qualify for organic certification?

a) 1 year b) 2 years

c) 3 years d) 4 years

72 Vermicompost is prepared by?

a) Animals b) worms

c) Bacteria d) Fungus

73 Organic Farming is a matter of giving back to nature what we take from it", is the saying of?

a) Fantilanan, 1990. b) IFOAM, 1972

c) FAO d) None of the above

74 What is the requirement of Organic Farming ?

a) Economical use of resources b) No use of resources

c) Sustainable use of resources d) All of the above

75 How would you use inorganic fertilizer in Organic Farming?

a) As a complementary component

b) As a supplementary component

c) As substitute

d) None of the above

76 Father of biodynamic farming is?

a) Rudolf steiner
b) Mokichi Okada
c) Bourne
d) Wingerden

77 Rishi Krishi is commonly practiced in

a) Bihar
b) Mahya Pradesh
c) Karnataka
d) Andhra Pradesh

78 Panchgavya consists of?

a) Five products of earthworm
b) Five products of cow
c) Five products of Tree
d) Five products of soil

79 Natural farming was developed by?

a) Kogl
b) Wingerden
c) Bourne
d) Mokichi Okada

80 National Centre of Organic farming is located at?

a) Ghaziabad
b) Hyderabad
c) Bhopal
d) Banglore

Answer Key

1	a	2	c	3	c	4	a	5	d	6	b	7	a
8	c	9	d	10	c	11	b	12	c	13	c	14	b
15	b	16	c	17	c	18	b	19	c	20	c	21	c
22	b	23	d	24	c	25	d	26	d	27	c	28	d
29	a	30	d	31	c	32	d	33	c	34	c	35	c
36	d	37	b	38	c	39	a	40	b	41	b	42	c
43	d	44	b	45	c	46	b	47	c	48	c	49	c
50	b	51	d	52	c	53	a	54	d	55	a	56	d
57	d	58	b	59	a	60	b	61	b	62	a	63	d
64	b	65	c	66	b	67	d	68	a	69	d	70	a
71	c	72	b	73	a	74	c	75	a	76	a	77	b
78	b	79	d	80	a								

11

Protected Cultivation

1 Which type of vegetable is often grown in shade net house?

a) Tomato
b) Lettuce
c) Radish
d) Cucumber

2 What is the primary advantage of greenhouse cultivation for vegetable production?

a) Increased exposure to natural elements
b) Protection from pests and diseases
c) Lower cost of production
d) Reduced need for irrigation

3 Simple and low cost structures for off season vegetable production in open field conditions?

a) Net house
b) Plastic Low tunnels
c) Lath house
d) Hot beds

4 What is the direct use of plastic tunnels

a) Plant propagation
b) Raising nursery
c) Vegetable production
d) None of the above

5 Shade houses are particularly very useful in.

a) Humid areas
b) Dry area
c) Cool area
d) All of the above

6 Which is the most inexpensive covering material?

a) Polythene
b) Polyesters
c) PVC film
d) Fiberglass

7 Which one of the following is a long lasting covering material than others?

a) Polythene
b) Polyesters
c) PVC film
d) Fiberglass

8 Lath house is very useful in..

a) Very warm regions b) Very cold regions

c) Rainy reasons d) All of the above

9 Which of the following is a key factor to consider when designing a greenhouse for vegetable cultivation ?

a) Maximizing outdoor ventilation b) Reducing humidity levels

c) Maximizing natural light d) Efficient temperature control

10 Which type of covering material is commonly used in greenhouse construction ?

a) Concrete b) Glass

c) Metal sheets d) Brick

11 Which vegetable crop is well suited for greenhouse cultivation due to its high value and temperature?

a) Tomato b) Chilli

c) Cabbage d) Spinach

12 Which method of irrigation is commonly used in greenhouse vegetable production?

a) Flood irrigation b) Drip irrigation

c) Furrow irrigation d) Sprinkler irrigation

13 What is the optimal relative humidity range for greenhouse vegetable cultivation ?

a) 10-20% b) 30-40%

c) 60-80% d) 90-100%

14 How can CO_2 enrichment benefit greenhouse vegetable crops ?

a) It reduces he need for water

b) It increases photosynthesis and crop yield

c) It prevents disease outbreaks

d) It helps control humidity

15 Which of the following is a common pest in greenhouse vegetable production?

a) Aphids b) Rodents

c) Mosquitoes d) Birds

16 Term for growing two or more crops in the same greenhouse space during different seasons?

a) Crop stacking b) Crop rotation

c) Intercropping d) Monoculture

17 Suitable plant type in tomato for greenhouse is?

a) Determinate b) Indeterminate

c) Both d) None

18 How many times more is the production in Poly houses as compared to Open field?

a) 2 times b) 3-4 times

c) 5-6 times d) Same as open field

19 The span type greenhouse has ?

a) 2 roof slopes b) 3 roof slopes

c) 4 roof slopes d) Multiple roof slopes

20 What type of radiation in greenhouse is important for photosynthesis?

a) Photosynthetically acive radiation b) Far infrared radiation

c) Near infrared radiation d) Ultraviolet radiation

21 What type of radiation in greenhouse causes greenhouse effect

a) Near infrared radiation b) UV radiation

c) Photosynthetically active radiation d) Far infared radiation

22 Open roof greenhouses were developed by

a) Art Van Wingerden b) Rudolf steiner

c) Mokichi Okada d) Kogl

23 Commercial greenhouse orientation is in which direction?

a) East-West b) North-South

c) North –East d) North-West

24 Automatic systems in greenhouse are used to control?

a) Temerature b) Lighting

c) Ventilation d) All of the above

25 Mist beds are ?

a) Seedling units b) Vegetable production units

c) Germination units d) Propagation units

26 Which vegetable is commonly grown in high tunnel for extended growing season?

a) Potato b) Corn

c) Tomato d) Cabbage

27 Which vegetable is well suited for hydroponic cultivation in greenhouse?

a) Carrots b) Ptatoes

c) Lettuce d) Onions

28 What is the purpose of using mulches in protected cultivation of vegetable crops?

a) Increase evaporation b) Reduce soil temperature

c) Enhance weed growth d) Promote soil erosion

29 Key consideration while choosing a site for protected vegetable cultivation is?

a) Soil erosion b) Proximity to water bodies

c) Adequate Sunlight d) Altitude above 2000 meters

30 Which type of protected cultivation structure provides a controlled environment for year round vegetable production

a) Cloche b) Cold Frame

c) Polyhouse d) Shade house

31 Which tomato variety is often preferred for protected cultivation due to its determinate growth habit?

a) Cherry tomatoes b) Roma tomatoes

c) Beefsteak tomatoes d) Heirloom tomatoes

32 What is the primary purpose of protected cultivation in lettuce farming?

a) Increasing water usage b) Protecting from frost

c) Enhancing natural pest control d) Reducing sunlight exposure

33 Which environmental factor is more easily controlled in protected lettuce cultivation compared to open-field cultivation?

a) Rainfall b) Temperature

c) Wind speed d) Soil composition

34 Which pest is often a concern in protected lettuce cultivation?

a) Butterflies b) Ladybugs

c) Aphids d) Earthworms

35 What is the benefit of using a controlled irrigation system in protected lettuce cultivation?

a) Prevents water requirement

b) Reduces the need for fertilizers

c) Provides consistent moisture to the crop

d) Attracts beneficial insects

36 How does protected cultivation affect the water requirements of chili plants?

a) Reduces water requirements

b) Increases water requirements

c) Has no effect on water requirements

d) Decreases sunlight exposure

37 Which environmental factor is critical for chili fruit setting and development in protected cultivation?

a) High wind speed

b) Low humidity

c) Adequate pollinators

d) High temperatures

38 Which irrigation method is often used in protected chili cultivation to minimize water contact with foliage and reduce disease risk?

a) Flood irrigation

b) Furrow irrigation

c) Drip irrigation

d) Sprinkler irrigation

39 In protected chili cultivation, what is the primary advantage of using an automated climate control system?

a) Reducing labor costs

b) Promoting weed growth

c) Increasing pest populations

d) Minimizing temperature control

40 What is the ideal temperature range for greenhouse vegetable cultivation?

a) 40-60°F (4-16°C)

b) 65-75°F (18-24°C)

c) 80-90°F (27-32°C)

d) 100-110°F (38-43°C)

41 Which of the following greenhouse structures is typically arched and has no vertical sidewalls?

a) Gable house

b) Quonset house

c) Lean-to house

d) Dome house

42 Which vegetable crop is often trained to grow vertically on trellises in a greenhouse ?

a) Cauliflower b) Zucchini

c) Cucumbers d) Onions

43 What is the main advantage of using raised beds in greenhouse vegetable production?

a) Improved drainage b) Reduced sunlight exposure

c) Lower heating costs d) Pest control

44 What is the primary purpose of a greenhouse's evaporative cooling system?

a) Reducing temperature b) Increasing humidity

c) Enhancing light diffusion d) Supporting trellising systems

45 Which greenhouse covering material is highly durable but expensive?

a) Polyethylene b) Polycarbonate

c) Shade cloth d) Glass

46 What is the primary benefit of using natural predators in greenhouse pest control?

a) Reduced plant growth b) Lower energy costs

c) Enhanced photosynthesis d) Increased fertilizer use

47 What is the purpose of using a humidification system in a greenhouse?

a) To reduce humidity levels b) To cool the greenhouse

c) To increase humidity levels d) To provide extra light

48 Which season is ideal for protected cultivation of cucurbits in most regions?

a) Winter b) Spring

c) Summer d) Fall

49 Which cucurbit crop is often trained to grow vertically in protected cultivation?

a) Zucchini b) Cucumber

c) Watermelon d) Pumpkin

50 Which cucurbit crop is best suited for high tunnel cultivation?

a) Watermelon b) Squash

c) Muskmelon d) Pumpkin

51 What is the ideal pH range for the soil in protected cucumber cultivation?

a) 5.0-6.0 b) 6.5-7.5

c) 8.0-9.0 d) 3.0-4.0

52 In protected cultivation, which method is used to enhance pollination in cucurbit crops?

a) Wind pollination b) Hand pollination

c) Insect pollination d) Self-pollination

53 Which disease is often controlled using resistant cucumber varieties in protected cultivation?

a) Powdery mildew b) Downy mildew

c) Fusarium wilt d) Root rot

54 What is the recommended spacing between cucumber plants in a greenhouse?

a) 6-12 inches (15-30 cm) b) 24-36 inches (61-91 cm)

c) 48-72 inches (122-183 cm) d) 96-120 inches (244-305 cm)

55 What is the recommended height of the greenhouse for cucumber cultivation?

a) 6 feet (1.8 meters) b) 12 feet (3.6 meters)

c) 20 feet (6 meters) d) 30 feet (9 meters)

56 What is the typical lifespan of cucumber plants in protected cultivation?

a) 1-2 years b) 3-4 months

c) 10-12 years d) 25-30 years

57 Which chili variety is commonly grown in greenhouses due to its sensitivity to temperature and climate?

a) Jalapeño b) Habanero

c) Bell pepper d) Thai bird's eye

58 Which vegetable crop is often grown in greenhouses due to its sensitivity to temperature and climate?

a) Carrots b) Peppers

c) Potatoes d) Cabbage

59 Which soil condition is preferable for chili plants in protected cultivation?

a) Alkaline soil b) Sandy soil

c) Loamy soil d) Compacted clay soil

60 What is the benefit of using a controlled environment in chili cultivation?

a) Reduced labor costs
b) Increased risk of pests and diseases
c) Extended growing seasons
d) Natural pollination

61 Which type of cover is often used for protecting chili plants from cold temperatures at night in greenhouses?

a) Shade net
b) Plastic sheeting
c) Straw mulch
d) Windbreak

62 Why is temperature control crucial for chili plants in protected cultivation?

a) To promote fruit ripening
b) To deter pests
c) To improve nutrient uptake
d) To prevent heat stress and cold damage

63 What is the purpose of using biological control agents in protected chili cultivation?

a) To encourage pests for natural balance
b) To promote plant growth
c) To manage pest populations
d) To reduce humidity

64 Which greenhouse structure is most commonly used for commercial vegetable production?

a) Quonset
b) Gable
c) Dome
d) Lean-to

65 Which type of greenhouse ventilation system is most energy-efficient?

a) Ridge ventilation
b) Roof exhaust fans
c) Side-wall ventilation
d) Louvered vents

66 What is the ideal relative humidity range for cucurbit cultivation in a greenhouse?

a) 20-30%
b) 50-70%
c) 80-90%
d) 95-100%

67 Which greenhouse covering material has good insulation properties?

a) Glass
b) Polycarbonate
c) Polyethylene
d) Shade cloth

68 Which vegetable crop is typically grown in a hanging basket in a greenhouse?

a) Kale
b) Lettuce
c) Strawberries
d) Radishes

69 Which greenhouse component is used to control temperature and humidity?

a) Shade net
b) Evaporative cooling system
c) Grow lights
d) Roof vent

70 What is the key advantage of using drip irrigation in greenhouse vegetable production?

a) Higher water use efficiency
b) Faster growth rate
c) Lower labor costs
d) Improved disease resistance

71 Which greenhouse gas is associated with the "greenhouse effect"?

a) Oxygen (O2)
b) Nitrogen (N2)
c) Carbon dioxide (CO2)
d) Hydrogen (H2)

72 What is the primary purpose of using trellising systems in greenhouse vegetable cultivation?

a) Improving nutrient uptake
b) Enhancing support for plants
c) Controlling pests
d) Increasing humidity

73 What is the purpose of using a shade net in a greenhouse?

a) Reducing light intensity and temperature
b) Increasing light intensity and temperature
c) Enhancing natural pollination
d) Controlling humidity

74 What is the night time temperature of cool green house?

a) 5 – 7°C
b) 10 – 12°C
c) 12 – 18°C
d) 7 – 10°C

75 What is the night time temperature of warm green house?

a) 8 – 12°C.
b) 10 – 13°C
c) 15 – 20°C
d) None of the above.

76 A walk in tunnel can withstand wind up to?

a) 120 km/hr
b) 90 km/hr
c) 150 km/hr
d) 200 km/hr

77 The main purpose of shade net house is..?

a) Hardening plants b) Plant propagation

c) Nursery raising d) All of the above

78 The optimum size of walk in tunnel is?

a) 40 – 50 square meter b) 60 – 75 square meter

c) 75 – 100 square meter d) 100 – 125 square mete

79 Which is mini green house?

a) Net house b) Low tunnel

c) Walk in tunnel d) Mist chamber

80 Which is also known as row cover?

a) Fluorescent Light chanmber b) Shade house

c) Walk in tunnel d) Low tunnel

Answer Key

1	b	2	b	3	b	4	c	5	b	6	a	7	b
8	a	9	b	10	b	11	a	12	b	13	d	14	c
15	a	16	c	17	d	18	b	19	b	20	c	21	a
22	b	23	b	24	b	25	c	26	c	27	b	28	a
29	a	30	b	31	c	32	b	33	b	34	c	35	c
36	b	37	a	38	c	39	a	40	c	41	d	42	b
43	a	44	d	45	a	46	c	47	d	48	a	49	d
50	a	51	c	52	b	53	c	54	b	55	b	56	c
57	c	58	b	59	c	60	a	61	a	62	c	63	b
64	b	65	b	66	a	67	c	68	c	69	c	70	d
71	a	72	c	73	c	74	b	75	d	76	c	77	a
78	c	79	b	80	c								

12

Exotic and Underutilized Vegetables

1 *Sechium eduleis* the botanical name of

a) Chekurmanis b) Basella

c) Chow-Chow d) Water Leaf

2 Cylon Spinach is also known as

a) Chayote b) Malabar Spinach

c) Indian Spinach d) Water Leaf

3 Botanical name of Leek is

a) Allium porum b) Allium sativum

c) Allium cepa d) None of these

4 Scientific name of Cylon Spinach is

a) *Talinum triangulare* b) *Sechium edule*

c) *Sauropus androgynus* d) *Basella alba*

5 Which of the following is known as "vegetable of 21st century"

a) Chow-Chow b) Chayote

c) Chekurmanis d) Leek

6 Chow-Chow belongs to family

a) Phyllanthaceae b) Cucurbitaceae

c) Basellaceae d) Alliaceae

7 Chinese Potato is also known as

a) Coleus b) Koorka

c) Both a and b d) None of these

8 Botanical name of Taro is

a) *Colocasia esculenta* b) *Maranta arundinacea*

c) *Eleocharis dulcis* d) *Helianthus tuberosus*

9 Green Mountain is a variety of

a) Sprouting Broccoli b) Brussels Sprout

c) Kale d) KnolKhol

10 Spine Gourd is also known as

a) Parwal b) Chayote

c) Kakrol d) Askas

11 Origin of Chow-Chow is

a) Asia b) Mexico

c) Africa d) India

12 Spine Gourd is

a) Monoecious b) Hermaphrodite

c) Dioecious d) Gynoecious

13 *Lactuca sativa* is the botanical name of

a) Chinese Cabbage b) Parsley

c) Celery d) Lettuce

14 Seed rate of Parsley is

a) 150-200 g/ha b) 250-300 g/ha

c) 350-400 g/ha d) 450-500 g/ha

15 Celery belongs to family

a) Compositae b) Cruciferae

c) Brassicaceae d) Apiaceae

16 Jerusalem Artichoke is a commercial source of

a) Glucose b) Fructose

c) Levulose d) Both a and b

17 Tender shoots of Asparagus are known as

a) Cuttings b) Spears

c) Suckers d) None of these

18 Botanical name of Globe Artichoke is

a) *Helianthus tuberosus* b) *Maranta arundinacea*

c) *Eleocharis dulcis* d) *Cynara scolymus*

19 Edible part of Globe Artichoke is

a) Flower bud b) Tubers

c) Petiole d) Thick leaf stalk

20 Edible part of Earth Apple is
a) Suckers
b) Tubers
c) Flower bud
d) Both a and b

21 Jerusalem Artichoke is also known as
a) Sunchoke
b) Earth Apple
c) Globe Artichoke
d) Both a and b

22 Colocasia is also known as
a) Arvi
b) Taro
c) Chinese Potato
d) Both a and b

23 Which of the following is a single seeded fruit
a) Chayote
b) Leek
c) Spine Gourd
d) Ivy Gourd

24 Chow-Chow is also known as
a) Kakrol
b) Chayote
c) Koorka
d) Arvi

25 London Flag is a variety of
a) Basella
b) Chow-Chow
c) Leek
d) Water Leaf

26 Botanical name of Chekurmanis is
a) *Helianthus tuberosus*
b) *Maranta arundinacea*
c) *Eleocharis dulcis*
d) *Sauropus androgynus*

27 Rhubarb is propagated by
a) Cuttings
b) Corms
c) Spears
d) Tubers

28 Propagation method of Globe Artichoke is
a) Suckers
b) Corms
c) Tubers
d) Cuttings

29 Origin of Asparagus is
a) Europe
b) Asia
c) Both a and b
d) None of these

30 White Asparagus is produced by
a) Steaming
b) Blanching
c) Boiling
d) Both c and d

31 Drum Stick belongs to family

a) Lilliaceae b) Compositae

c) Moringaceae d) Moraceae

32 Principal carbohydrate present in the tubers of Jerusalem artichoke is

a) Glucofractons b) Glucoraphanin

c) Sulforaphane d) None of these

33 Scientific name of Chinese Potato is

a) *Helianthus tuberosus* b) *Maranta arundinacea*

c) *Eleocharis dulcis* d) *Solenostemon rotundifolium*

34 Chinese Potato is native of

a) India b) Africa

c) Asia d) Brazil

35 Edible part of Celery is

a) Thick petiole b) Flower bud

c) Fleshy leaf stalk d) Tubers

36 Plain leafed, double curled and moss curled are three types of

a) Celery b) Parsley

c) Lettuce d) Kale

37 Spine Gourd is propagated by

a) Tuberous roots b) Root cuttings

c) Limb Cuttings d) Both b and c

38 Vivipary is the propagation method of

a) Spine Gourd b) Ridge Gourd

c) Sponge Gourd d) Chow-Chow

39 Kale belongs to family

a) Umbeliferae b) Lilliaceae

c) Cruciferae d) Alliaceae

40 Type of inflorescence in Broccoli is

a) Racemose b) Cymose

c) Raceme d) Umbel

41 Rich source of sulphoraphane is

a) Kale
b) Broccoli
c) Lettuce
d) Brussels Sprout

42 Thermodormancy is found in

a) Parsley
b) Celery
c) Lettuce
d) Kale

43 Lettuce is a _________ crop

a) Cross-pollinated
b) Often cross pollinated
c) Self-pollinated
d) Both b and c

44 Botanical name of Celery is

a) *Apium graveolens*
b) *Maranta arundinacea*
c) *Eleocharis dulcis*
d) *Solenostemon rotundifolium*

45 Great Lakes is a variety of

a) Celery
b) Lettuce
c) Parsley
d) Kale

46 *Petroselinum crispum* is the botanical name of

a) Parsley
b) Celery
c) Chinese Cabbage
d) Kale

47 Exposure to high temperature in Celery causes

a) Yellowing of leaves
b) Bitterness in leaves
c) Drying of leaf stalks
d) Defoliation

48 Chinese Potato is propagated by

a) Vine cuttings
b) Suckers
c) Tubers
d) All of these

49 Colocasia belongs to family

a) Lamaiaceae
b) Moraceae
c) Araceae
d) Asteraceae

50 Sree Dhara is a variety of

a) Globe Artichoke
b) Moringa
c) Chinese Potato
d) Rhubarb

51 Moringa is also known as

a) Kakrol
b) Drum Stick
c) Coleus
d) Taro

52 Optimum pH requirement for cultivation of Asparagus is

a) 4.5-5.5
b) 5.5-6.5
c) 6.0-6.7
d) 7.0-7.7

53 Most serious disease of Asparagus is

a) Powdery mildew
b) Asparagus rot
c) Downy mildew
d) Anthracnose

54 Tudella is a variety of

a) Drum Stick
b) Asparagus
c) Globe Artichoke
d) Rhubarb

55 Spears of Asparagus contain

a) Asparagine
b) Levulose
c) Both a and b
d) None of these

56 Botanical name of Drum Stick is

a) *Atrocarpus altilis*
b) *Cynara scolymus*
c) *Rheum rhaponticum*
d) *Moringa oleifera*

57 Flower colour of Drum Stick is

a) Yellow
b) White
c) Blue
d) Pink

58 Asparagus take how many years for the real yield

a) 2
b) 3
c) 4
d) 5

59 Drum Stick is propagated by

a) Limb cuttings
b) Seeds
c) Tubers
d) Both a and b

60 Drum Stick is commercially grown in

a) Haryana
b) Maharashtra
c) Tamil Nadu
d) Madhya Pradesh

61 Origin of Leek is

a) Africa | b) South America
c) Asia | d) Europe

62 Origin of Cylon Spinach is

a) Mexico | b) South America
c) New Zealand | d) Brazil

63 Chow-Chow is a good source of

a) Vitamin A | b) Vitamin C
c) Vitamin D | d) Vitamin E

64 Which of the following is known as "Multivitamin greens"

a) Chow-Chow | b) Cylon Spinach
c) Chekurmanis | d) Basella

65 Bull is a variety of

a) Chekurmanis | b) Basella
c) Globe Artichoke | d) Rhubarb

66 Jaffna is a variety of

a) Asparagus | b) Moringa
c) Rhubarb | d) Chekurmanis

67 Satamukhi is a variety of

a) Chinese Potato | b) Yam Bean
c) Taro | d) Moringa

68 Florida Golden is a variety of

a) Moringa | b) Taro
c) Parsley | d) Celery

69 Lettuce is native of

a) Africa | b) Mediterranean region
c) Asia | d) Europe

70 Coastal Atlantic is a variety of

a) Broccoli | b) Kale
c) Lettuce | d) None of these

71 Globe artichoke is a _________ plant

a) C_3 b) C_4

c) CAM d) Both b and c

72 Seed rate of Drum Stick is

a) 300 g/ha b) 400 g/ha

c) 500 g/ha d) 600 g/ha

73 Four angled bean is the common name of

a) Broad Bean b) Winged Bean

c) Dolichos Bean d) Yam Bean

74 Toxic substance present in Celery is

a) Oxalic acid b) Haemaglutine

c) Serotonin d) Apiin

75 Largest producer of Broccoli is

a) USA b) India

c) China d) Nigeria

76 Suitable age for transplanting lettuce seedlings is

a) 6-8 weeks b) 4-5 weeks

c) 3-4 weeks d) None of these

77 Rooting depth of Asparagus is

a) 15-30 cm b) 120-180 cm

c) 80-100 cm d) None of these

78 Protoandry is present in

a) Asparagus b) Taro

c) Celery d) Sweet Corn

79 Isolation distance for certified seed in Lettuce is

a) 50 m b) 25 m

c) 100 m d) 200 m

80 Isolation distance for foundation seed in Lettuce is

a) 25 m b) 50 m

c) 200 m d) 400 m

81 Which of the following is a short-day plant

a) Spinach
b) Sweet Pepper
c) Cow Pea
d) Winged Bean

82 Optimum temperature requirement for cultivation of Lettuce is

a) 25-27 ºC
b) 20-25 ºC
c) 18-25 ºC
d) 10-15 ºC

83 Chromosome number of Rhubarb is

a) 24
b) 34
c) 44
d) 54

84 Botanical name of New Zealand Spinach is

a) *Tetragonia tetragonioides*
b) *Basella rubra*
c) *Paurus nobilis*
d) *Manihot esculenta*

85 Edible part of New Zealand Spinach is

a) Leaves
b) Tender leaves and tops
c) Green pods
d) Tender seeds

86 Botanical name of Agathi is

a) *Sesbania grandiflora*
b) *Basella rubra*
c) *Paurus nobilis*
d) *Manihot esculenta*

87 Edible part of Agathi is

a) Pods
b) Seeds
c) Flower
d) Leaves

88 Botanical name of winged Bean is

a) *Sesbania grandiflora*
b) *Basella rubra*
c) *Paurus nobilis*
d) *Psophocarpus tetragonolobus*

89 Chromosome number of winged bean is

a) 12
b) 16
c) 18
d) 20

90 Chromosome number of Celery is

a) 16
b) 18
c) 22
d) 24

91 New Zealand Spinach belongs to family

a) Polygonaceae b) Azioaceae

c) Lauraceae d) Malvaceae

92 Chromosome number of Chive is

a) 10 b) 12

c) 14 d) 16

93 Shallot belongs to family

a) Araceae b) Alliaceae

c) Graminae d) Lilliaceae

94 Edible part of Broccoli is

a) Curd b) Head

c) Flower bud d) Knob

95 *Cucumis anguriais* the scientific name of

a) Cucumber b) Long Melon

c) Snap Melon d) Gherkin

96 Origin of *Cucumis anguria* is

a) Tropical America b) Tropical Africa

c) Asia d) Mexico

97 Chromosome number of Ivy Gourd is

a) 22 b) 24

c) 32 d) 40

98 Chromosome number of Shallot is

a) 10 b) 12

c) 16 d) 20

99 Chromosome number of Asparagus is

a) 20 b) 18

c) 16 d) 14

100 Edible part of Lettuce is

a) Leaves b) Stem

c) Leafy heads d) Flower bud

101 Chromosome number of Lettuce is

a) 26 b) 18

c) 12 d) 10

102 Botanical name of Broccoli is

a) *Brassica oleracea var. botrytis*

b) *Brassica oleracea var. gemmifera*

c) *Brassica oleracea var. italica*

d) *Brassica oleracea var. gongylodes*

103 Chromosome number of Gherkin is

a) 12 b) 24

c) 36 d) 44

104 Botanical name of Asparagus is

a) *Sesbania grandiflora* b) *Basella rubra*

c) *Paurus nobilis* d) *Asparagus officinalis*

105 Origin of Globe Artichoke is

a) Mediterranean region b) Tropical Asia

b) Tropical Africa d) Brazil

106 Edible part of Gherkin is

a) Leaves b) Stem

c) Fruit d) Curd

107 Botanical name of Ivy Gourd is

a) *Sesbania grandiflora* b) *Coccinia indica*

c) *Paurus nobilis* d) *Asparagus officinalis*

108 Chinese Potato belongs to family

a) Labitae b) Malvaceae

c) Convolvulaceae d) Solanaceae

109 Cherry Tomato belongs to family

a) Convolvulaceae b) Solanaceae

c) Malvaceae d) Lilliaceae

110 *Solanum lycopersicum var. cerasiforme* is the botanical name of

a) Tomato b) Potato

c) Brinjal d) Cherry Tomato

111 Tiny Tim is an early-maturing cultivar of

a) Tomato b) Brinjal

c) Cherry Tomato d) None of these

112 Malic acid is present in

a) Tomato b) Cherry Tomato

c) Lettuce d) Potato

113 Which of the following is not a variety of Broccoli

a) Green Head b) Decicco

c) Geen Bud d) Scotish

114 Kale belongs to family

a) Compositae b) Malvaceae

c) Cruciferae d) Lilliaceae

115 Crisphead is a type of

a) Cabbage b) Broccoli

c) Cauliflower d) Lettuce

116 Seeds of Lettuce do not germinate when the temperature is above

a) 18 °C b) 20 °C

c) 22 °C d) 24 °C

117 Bolting in Celery takes place when the temperature is below

a) 15 °C b) 20 °C

c) 25 °C d) None of these

118 Taro is propagated by

a) Corms b) Cormels

c) Tubers d) Suckers

119 Fruit weight of Drum Stick is

a) 150 g b) 230 g

c) 320 g d) 300 g

120 Valentine is a variety of

a) Drum Stick b) Taro

c) Lettuce d) Rhubarb

121 Rhubarb belongs to family

a) Polygonaceae b) Asteraceae

c) Compositae d) Lilliaceae

122 Pie Plant is another name for

a) Chinese Cabbage b) Celery

c) Parsley d) Rhubarb

123 Botanical name of Chinese Cabbage is

a) *Brassica oleraceae* b) *Brassica chinensis*

c) *Brassica campestris* d) None of these

124 China is the origin of

a) Lettuce b) Spinach

c) Chinese Cabbage d) Taro

125 Botanical name of Rhubarb is

a) *Cynara scolymus* b) *Rheum rhaponticum*

c) *Atrocarpus altilis* d) None of these

126 Hilds Ideal is a variety of

a) Broccoli b) Chinese Cabbage

c) Brussels Sprout d) Kale

127 Bitterness is Brussels Sprouts is imparted by excessive application of

a) Potash b) Urea

c) Ammonium Nitrate d) Phosphorus

128 Mini Cabbage is another name for

a) Chinese Cabbage b) Broccoli

c) Brussels Sprouts d) Lettuce

129 Chinese Yellow is a variety of

a) Chinese Cabbage b) Brussels Sprouts

c) Broccoli d) Lettuce

130 Pencil Strip disease of Celery is due to excess

a) Nitrogen b) Potassium

c) Phosphorus d) Calcium

131 Cracked stem in celery is due to deficiency of

a) Calcium
b) Boron
c) Phosphorus
d) None of these

132 Asparagus is propagated by

a) Corms
b) Cormels
c) Spears
d) Seeds

133 Mcdonold is a variety of

a) Asparagus
b) Celery
c) Rhubarb
d) Chinese Cabbage

134 Which of the following is a cold resistant plant

a) Asparagus
b) Globe Artichoke
c) Sunchoke
d) Rhubarb

135 Adzuki bean is the common name of

a) *Vigna angularis*
b) *Vigna unguiculata*
c) *Vicia faba*
d) *Vigna umbelata*

136 *Canavalia gladiate* is the scientific name of

a) Broad Bean
b) Winged Bean
c) Lima Bean
d) Sword Bean

137 Flower colour of Winged Bean is

a) Blue
b) White
c) Purple
d) All of these

138 The pods of Winged Bean are_______sided

a) 3
b) 4
c) 6
d) None of these

139 *Canavalia ensiformis* is the botanical name of

a) Sword Bean
b) Winged Bean
c) French Bean
d) Jack Bean

140 Haricot bean is the common name of

a) *Vigna angularis*
b) *Vigna unguiculata*
c) *Vicia faba*
d) *Vigna umbelata*

141 Botanical name of Zucchini is

a) *Cucurbita pepo*
b) *Cucurbita maxima*
c) *Cucurbita moshcata*
d) None of these

142 Pusa Alankar is the F1 hybrid of

a) Summer Squash
b) Pumpkin
c) Winter Squash
d) Chow-Chow

143 Harvesting stage of Zucchini is

a) $1/2^{nd}$ maturity
b) $1/3^{rd}$ maturity
c) $1/4^{th}$ maturity
d) None the above

144 Black heart of Celery is due to the deficiency of

a) Boron
b) Calcium
c) Potassium
d) Phosphorus

145 Rosettee spotting in lettuce is caused by ______ injury

a) Ethylene
b) Mechanical
c) Frost
d) None of these

146 Early Yellow prolific is a variety of

a) Chow-Chow
b) Summer Squash
c) Ivy Gourd
d) Pumpkin

147 Tip burn of Lettuce is caused by

a) Ca deficiency + unfavourable climate
b) Boron deficiency + frost injury
c) Ca deficiency
d) Boron deficiency

148 Baby marrow is another name for

a) Artichoke
b) Celery
c) Zucchini
d) Rhubarb

149 Type of inflorescence in celery is

a) Cymose
b) Corymb
c) Spadix
d) Umbel

150 Agathi is a rich source of

a) Calcium
b) Potassium
c) Phosphorus
d) Sulphur

Answer Key

1	c	2	d	3	a	4	a	5	c	6	b	7	c
8	a	9	a	10	c	11	b	12	c	13	d	14	b
15	d	16	c	17	b	18	d	19	a	20	b	21	d
22	d	23	a	24	b	25	c	26	d	27	b	28	a
29	c	30	b	31	c	32	a	33	d	34	b	35	c
36	b	37	a	38	d	39	c	40	b	41	b	42	c
43	c	44	a	45	b	46	a	47	b	48	d	49	c
50	c	51	b	52	c	53	b	54	c	55	a	56	d
57	b	58	b	59	d	60	c	61	b	62	d	63	b
64	c	65	c	66	b	67	c	68	d	69	b	70	a
71	b	72	c	73	b	74	d	75	a	76	b	77	b
78	c	79	b	80	b	81	d	82	c	83	c	84	a
85	b	86	a	87	c	88	d	89	c	90	c	91	b
92	d	93	b	94	c	95	d	96	b	97	b	98	c
99	a	100	c	101	b	102	c	103	b	104	d	105	a
106	c	107	b	108	a	109	b	110	d	111	c	112	c
113	d	114	c	115	d	116	c	117	a	118	b	119	b
120	d	121	a	122	d	123	b	124	c	125	b	126	c
127	a	128	c	129	d	130	c	131	b	132	c	133	c
134	d	135	a	136	d	137	d	138	b	139	d	140	d
141	a	142	a	143	b	144	b	145	a	146	b	147	a
148	c	149	d	150	a								

13

Growth and Development

1 Choose the correct option for the characteristic of growth.

a) It is an irreversible permanent increase in size of an organ or its parts or even of an individual cell

b) It is accompanied by metabolic processes

c) It occurs at the expense of energy

d) All of the above

2 Plant growth is unique because

a) Plants bear the capacity for unlimited growth

b) Plants bear the capacity for limited growth

c) Plants have diffused growth that differs from animals

d) None of the above

3 The cells of ________ have the capacity to divide and self-perpetuate.

a) Permanent tissue b) Quiescent centre

c) Meristems d) Subapical part

4 The type of growth where new cells are always being added to the plant body by the activity of meristem is called

a) closed form of growth b) diffused form of growth

c) open form of growth d) discontinuous form of growth

5 Primary growth of plants is contributed by

a) root apical meristem b) shoot apical meristem

c) Both (a) and (b) d) None of these

6 The tissues responsible for secondary growth in plants are?

a) vascular cambium b) cork cambium

c) lateral meristem d) All of these

7 Growth at cellular level is the increase in the amount of

a) Cell wall
b) Cell membrane
c) Protoplasm
d) All of these

8 The period of growth does not include

a) Meristematic phase
b) Elongation phase
c) Death phase
d) Maturation phase

9 Constantly dividing cells, both at the root apex and shoot apex represent

a) Elongation phase of the growth
b) Meristematic phase of the growth
c) Maturation phase of the growth
d) None of the above

10 The cells in the root and shoot apex

a) Are rich in protoplasm
b) Have conspicuous nuclei with abundant plasmodesmatal connections
c) Have cell walls which are primary in nature, thin and cellulosic
d) All of the above

11 The cells proximal (just next away from the tip) to the meristematic zone represent the phase of

a) Division
b) Maturation
c) Elongation
d) Differentiation

12 Arithmetic growth is linear because

a) One daughter cell remains meristematic and other differentiates and mature
b) Both daughter cells remain meristematic
c) Both daugther cells get matured
d) All of the above

13 In geometrical growth, lag phase is represented by

a) Initial rapid growth
b) Later rapid growth
c) Initial slow growth
d) Later slow growth

14 In geometrical growth, exponential phase is represented by?

a) Rapid consumption of nutrients
b) Rapid increase in cell number
c) Highest growth rate
d) All of the above

15 Typical growth curve in plants is

a) Sigmoid
b) linear
c) Stair-steps-shaped
d) Parabolic

16 In geometrical growth (from beginning to last) the correct sequence of growth phases and their occurrence are I. lag phase II. stationary phase III. exponential phase

a) I → II → III
b) I → III → II
c) III → II → I
d) III → I → II

17 Grand phase or the fastest phase of growth in S-shaped growth curve is

a) lag phase
b) Stationary phase.
c) Diminishing growth phase
d) Exponential growth phase.

18 Efficiency index in the geometrical growth is the ability of plants to produce

a) Cell wall
b) New enzyme
c) New plant material
d) Young ones through mitosis

19 Developing embryo (in vitro) shows

a) Geometric growth
b) Arithmetic growth
c) Logistic growth
d) Both (a) and (b)

20 Quantitative comparisons between the growth of living system can be made in

a) Two ways
b) Three ways
c) Only one way
d) Four ways

21 Measurement and comparison of total growth of a plant per unit time is called

a) Absolute growth rate
b) Qualitative growth rate
c) Relative growth rate
d) Exponential growth rate

22 Auxanometer is used to measure

a) Growth in the length of plant organ
b) Growth in the width of plant organ
c) Population of the pest-attacking plants
d) Both (a) and (b)

23 Which of the following are the factors for plant growth?

a) Water and O2

b) Light, temperature and gravity

c) Nutrients

d) All of the above

24 Water is required in plant growth for

a) Enzymatic reactions b) Cell enlargement

c) Extension growth d) All of these

25 The living differentiated cells, regain the capacity of division under certain conditions which is called

a) Redifferentiation b) Dedifferentiation

c) Differentiation d) Reverse division

26 The formation of which of the following is the example of de-differentiation?

a) Procambium and vascular cambium

b) Cork cambium and interfascicular cambium

c) Cork cambium and vascular cambium

d) Procambium and cork cambium

27 If a part of pith from the stem of a plant is used as an explant and cultured on nutrient medium, which of the following processes is responsible for the formation of an undifferentiated mass of cells called callus?

a) Growth b) Differentiation

c) Dedifferentiation d) Redifferentiation

28 Name the process when dedifferentiated cells again loss the ability to divide and get mature

a) Cell enlargement b) Redifferentiation

c) Dedifferentiation d) Differentiation

29 Growth of the plant is

a) Determinate b) Indeterminate

c) Continuous d) Both (a) and (b)

30 The final structure at maturity of a cell/tissue is determined by

a) Type of cells b) Type of cell division

c) location of cells within the tissue d) Nutrients in cells

31 The term that includes a series of changes that an organism goes through during its life cycle from germination of the seed to senescence is

a) Maturation
b) Development
c) Growth
d) Differentiation

32 Identify the correct sequence from the following events of development process in a plant cell choose the correct option. I. Plasmatic growth II. Differentiation III. Maturation IV. Senescence

a) I ⟶ II ⟶ III ⟶ IV
b) I ⟶ II ⟶ IV ⟶ III
c) IV ⟶ III ⟶ II ⟶ I
d) IV ⟶ I ⟶ II ⟶ III

33 The ability of plants to follow different pathways to form different structure in response to the environment is called

a) Plasticity
b) Elasticity
c) Growth
d) Development

34 When transition from juvenile to adult is gradual then this type of development is called

a) Homoblastic development
b) Heteroblastic development
c) Homo and heteroblastic development
d) Hetero and homoblastic development

35 The study of different aspects or appearances of plants in different seasons of the year is called

a) Ecology
b) Ecosystem
c) Phenology
d) Demography

36 Which of them are not extrinsic factors for growth of plants?

a) Light, O2
b) Temperature, CO2
c) Nutrient, water
d) Growth regulator and genetic factor

37 Which one includes growth promoters?

a) Auxin, cytokinin, ABA
b) GA, cytokinin, C H2 4
c) C H2 2, ABA
d) Auxin, cytokinin, GA3

38 Which one includes growth inhibitors?

a) ABA, cytokinin
b) GA, IAA
c) ABA4, C H2
d) None of the above

39 Canary grass experiment for phototropism was first conducted by

a) Went
b) Darwin and Darwin
c) Cousins
d) Kurosawa

40 Hormone involved in phototropism is

a) Auxin
b) Gibberelin
c) Kinetin
d) 2, 4-D

41 In coleoptile tissue, auxin is

a) Not transported because it used where it is made
b) Transported by diffusion
c) Transported from base to tip by as mosses
d) Produced by growing apices of stem which migrate to the region of its action

42 'Bakanae' (foolish seedling) disease of rice seedlings, was caused by Gibberella fujikuroi, which is a

a) Fungi
b) Protozoan
c) Bacteria
d) Virus

43 You are given a tissue with its potential for differentiation in an artificial culture. Which of the following pairs of hormones would you add to the medium to secure shoots as well as roots?

a) IAA and gibberellin
b) Auxin and cytokinin
c) Auxin and abscisic acid
d) Gibberellin and abscisic acid

44 Cytokinesis promoting active substance kinetin identified and crystallised by

a) Skoog and Miller
b) Cousins.
c) E Kurosawa
d) Darwin.

45 The Plant Growth Regulator (PGR), ethylene is

a) Volatile
b) Gaseous in nature
c) Both (a) and (b)
d) None of these.

46 Which hormone was first isolated from human urine?

a) Auxin
b) ABA.
c) Ethylene
d) Gibberellic acid.

47 Movement of auxin is

a) Basipetal
b) Acropetal.
c) Centripetal
d) Both (a) and (b)

48 High concentration of auxin is present in

a) Root apex
b) Stem apex.
c) Node
d) Petiole.

49 Natural and synthetic auxins (IAA, NAA, IBA, 2,4-D) have been used extensively in

a) Agriculture
b) Horticulture.
c) Sericulture
d) Both (a) and (b).

50 Which of the following effects of auxins on plants is the basis for their commercial application?

a) Callus formation
b) Curvature of stem.
c) Induction of root formation in stem cuttings
d) Induction of shoot formation.

51 Fruit and leaf drop at early stages can be prevented by the application of

a) Cytokinins
b) Ethylene.
c) Auxins
d) Gibberellic acid.

52 Removal of auxin source demonstrates that leaf abscission is ____ by auxin and apical dominance is ___ by auxin.

a) Promoted, promoted
b) Inhibited, inhibited.
c) Promoted, inhibited
d) Inhibited, promoted.

53 Removal of shoot tips is very useful technique to boost the production of tea leaves. This is because

a) Gibberellins prevent bolting and are inactivated.
b) Auxins prevent leaf drop at early stages.
c) Effect of auxins is removed and growth of lateral buds is enhanced
d) Gibberellins delay senescence of leaves.

54 Parthenocarpy in tomatoes is induced by

a) Cytokinin b) Auxin.

c) Gibberellin d) Ethylene.

55 Which of the following is not a plant growth inhibitor?

a) Dormin b) IAA.

c) Ethylene d) ABA.

56 The plant hormone produced by Rhizobium for nodulation is

a) IBA b) NAA.

c) 2, 4-D d) IAA.

57 How many gibberellins are reported from different organisms such as plants and fungi?

a) More than 50 b) More than 75.

c) More than 100 d) More than 25.

58 Which one of the following is not an effect of gibberellin?

a) Increase the length of grapes stalks.

b) Delay senescence of fruits.

c) Induce dormancy

d) Increase the length of sugarcane stem.

59 During seed germination, its stored food is mobilised by

a) Ethylene b) Cytokinin.

c) ABA d) Gibberellin.

60 Specific property attributed to GA is

a) Shortening of genetically tall plants

b) Elongation of genetically dwarf plants.

c) Rooting or stem cuttings

d) Promotion of leaf and fruit fall.

61 Internodal elongation just prior to flowering in sugarbeet, cabbage and in many plants with rosette habit is called

a) Pruning b) Bolting.

c) Grafting d) Cutting.

62 Cytokinins are mostly

a) Glucosides b) Phenolics.

c) Amino purines d) Organic acids.

63 Difference between kinetin and zeatin is

a) Kinetin is active, while zeatin is non-active.

b) Zeatin is active, while kinetin is non-active.

c) Zeatin is synthetic, while kinetin is natural

d) Zeatin is natural, while kinetin is synthetic.

64 Natural cytokinins are synthesised in regions where rapid cell division occurs such regions are

a) Root apices
b) Young fruit
c) Developing shoot buds
d) All of these

65 Which hormone (PGR) encounters apical dominance induced by auxin?

a) IAA
b) Cytokinin
c) C H2 4
d) NAA

66 The problem of necrosis and gradual senescence, while performing tissue culture can be overcome by

a) Spraying auxins
b) Spraying cytokinins
c) Suspension culture
d) Subculture

67 Cytokinin helps in delaying the leaf falling/senescence mainly by

a) Promoting nutrient mobilisation
b) Inhibiting cell division
c) Promoting cell elongation
d) Promoting cell differentiation

68 Which plant hormone is found in gaseous form?

a) Auxin
b) Cytokinin
c) Ethylene
d) ABA

69 Large amount of ethylene is synthesised by

a) Developing roots and fruits

b) Developing shoots and flowers

c) Tissues undergoing senescence and ripening fruits

d) Young tissue and unripened fruits

70 Respiratory climacteric is related with

a) ABA
b) Ethylene
c) Auxin
d) GA

71 Surface area of roots by promoting root growth and root hair formation is increased by

a) Cytokinin
b) Kinetin
c) Ethylene
d) ABA

72 Most widely used compound as a source of ethylene is

a) Nepthol
b) Acetol
c) Ethephon
d) Ethepcon

73 Ethephon?

a) Hastens fruit ripening in tomatoes
b) Accelerates abscission
c) Increases number of female flowers in cucumber
d) All of the above

74 A farmer grows cucumber plants in his field. He wants to increase the number of female flowers in them. Which plant growth regulator can be applied to achieve this?

a) ABA
b) Ethylene
c) GA
d) Cytokinins

75 The shedding of leaves, flowers and fruits due to changes in hormonal levels in plants, is referred to as

a) Senescence
b) Abscission
c) Photoperiodism
d) Vernalisation

76 In response to biotic and abiotic stress, growth inhibition activities are caused by

a) ABA
b) Ethylene
c) IAA
d) IBA

77 Which one of the following growth regulators is known as 'stress hormone'?

a) Abscisic acid
b) Ethylene
c) GA3
d) Indole acetic acid

78 In most situations, ABA acts

a) Agonist to auxin
b) Antagonist to gibberellin
c) Antagonist to auxin
d) Agonist to gibberellin

79 Which organelle synthesises the abscisic acid?

a) Golgi body
b) ER
c) Lysosome
d) Chloroplast

109 Abscisic acid

a) Inhibits seed germination
b) Stimulates closure of stomata
c) Induces seed dormancy
d) All of the above

80 In plants, phototropism is the movement

a) Towards the light source
b) Away from the light source
c) Parallel to the light source
d) Lateral to the light source

81 Plants which require exposure to light for a period greater than critical day length are

a) Long day plants
b) Long-short day plants
c) Short day plants
d) Short-long day plants

82 Short day plants require light for a period

a) Less than critical duration
b) Equal than critical duration
c) More than critical duration
d) Independent of critical duration

83 Day neutral plants

a) Show no flowering in any photoperiod
b) Show loss of activity during day time
c) Have no correlation between exposure to light duration and induction of flowering response
d) None of the above

84 Effect of daily duration of light and dark periods on growth and development of plants especially on flowering is called

a) Vernalisation
b) Photoperiodism
c) Phototaxis
d) Both (a) and (b)

85 Short day plant also called

a) Short night plant
b) Long night plant
c) Intermediate night plant
d) None of these

86 What is the site of perception of photoperiod necessary for induction of flowering in plants?

a) Pulvinus
b) Shoot apex
c) Leaves
d) Lateral buds

87 Choose the correct option.

a) Flowering in certain plants depends on a combination of light and dark exposures on plant.

b) Shoot apices of plant themselves cannot perceive photoperiods, they modify themselves into flowering apices prior to flowering.

c) There is a hormonal substance that is responsible for flowering

d) All of the above.

88 A long day plant having a critical photoperiod of 13 hours will flower in which condition? Duration of light period Duration of dark period

a) 13 11
b) 11 13
c) 12 12
d) 10 14

89 Which pigment is involved in photoperiodic changes in plants?

a) Phytochrome
b) Chlorophyll
c) Cytochrome
d) Anthocyanin

90 A few normal seedlings of tomato were kept in a dark room. After a few days they were found to have become white like albinos. Which of the following terms will you use to describe them?

a) Mutated
b) Embilised
c) Etiolated
d) Defoliated

91 Vernalisation is

a) Low pH treatment
b) Low temperature treatment
c) High temperature treatment
d) High pH treatment

92 Temperature required for vernalisation is

a) 5-10°C
b) 5-15°C
c) 0-5°C
d) 3-17°C

93 Through their effect on plant growth regulators, what do the temperature and light control in the plants

a) Apical dominance
b) Flowering
c) Closure of stomata
d) Fruit elongation

94 Hormone, which replaces the requirement of vernalisation is

a) Ethylene
b) Auxin
c) Gibberellin
d) Cytokinin

95 Examples of plants which require vernalisation is/are

a) Pea
b) Sugarbeet
c) Cabbage
d) All of these

96 Vernalisation can be reversed by

a) Application of high temperature
b) Application of auxin
c) Application of more less temperature
d) Application of gibberellin

97 Vernalisation stimulates flowering in

a) Jimikand
b) Turmeric
c) Carrot
d) Ginger

98 Stimulus of vernalisation is perceived by

a) Shoot tips
b) Mature tissues.
c) Embryo tips
d) Both (a) and (c)

99 Certain seeds which fail to germinate even when external conditions are favourable is due to

a) Photoperiodism
b) Seed dormancy
c) Vernalisation
d) Plasticity

100 Which of the following is/are factor causing seed dormancy?

a) Impermeable and hard seed coat
b) Chemical inhibitors like abscisic acids, phenolic acids and para-ascorbic acids
c) Immature embryos
d) All of the above

Answer Key

1	d	2	a	3	c	4	c	5	c	6	d	7	c
8	c	9	b	10	d	11	c	12	a	13	c	14	d
15	a	16	b	17	d	18	c	19	d	20	a	21	a
22	a	23	d	24	d	25	b	26	b	27	c	28	b
29	d	30	c	31	d	32	a	33	b	34	a	35	c
36	d	37	d	38	c	39	b	40	a	41	d	42	a
43	b	44	a	45	c	46	a	47	d	48	b	49	d
50	c	51	c	52	d	53	c	54	b	55	b	56	d
57	c	58	c	59	b	60	d	61	b	62	c	63	d
64	d	65	b	66	b	67	a	68	c	69	c	70	b
71	c	72	c	73	d	74	b	75	b	76	a	77	a
78	b	79	d	80	b	81	a	82	a	83	c	84	b
85	b	86	c	87	d	88	a	89	a	90	c	91	b
92	c	93	c	94	b	95	c	96	a	97	c	98	d
99	b	100	d										

14

Spices and Condiments

1 What is the scientific name of Dill

a) *Acorus calamus*
b) *Pimenta dioca*
c) *Pimpinella anisum*
d) *Anethum graveolens*

2 Important chemical content present in Asafoetida is

a) Phenol
b) Terbein
c) Ferumine
d) Limone

3 Karimunda is a variety of

a) Ginger
b) Black Pepper
c) Cardemom
d) Cumin

4 Which spice crop is known as "Queen of spices"

a) Large Cardamom
b) Small Cardamom
c) Black Pepper
d) Turmeric

5 What is the botanical name of Large Cardamom

a) Amomom subulatum
b) Elettaria cardamomum
c) Curcuma longa
d) None of these

6 What is the chromosome number of ginger

a) 48
b) 18
c) 22
d) 24

7 Good quality oleoresin can be extracted from

a) Black Pepper
b) Coriander
c) Fenugreek
d) Vanilla

8 Large Cardamom is propagated by

a) Seeds
b) Suckers
c) Roots
d) None of these

9 Economic part of Saffron is

a) Fruit b) Seed

c) Stigma d) Leaves

10 Cinnamon is native of

a) India b) Indo-Burma

c) Indonesia d) Sri Lanka

11 Bishop's weed belongs to which family

a) Rutaceae b) Lauraceae

c) Apiaceae d) None of these

12 What is the origin of All spice

a) South America b) West Indies

c) USA d) Europe

13 Which spice crop is known as "King of spices"

a) Cumin b) Cardamom

c) Black Pepper d) Turmeric

14 Which is the second most important spice next to Black pepper in the world

a) Nutmeg b) Kokum

c) Clove d) Fennel

15 Which is the most expensive spice in the world

a) Thyme b) Curry Leaf

c) Fennel d) Saffron

16 What is the scientific name of Thyme

a) *Ferulla foetida* b) *Thymus vulgaris*

c) *Juniperous communis* d) *Garcinia indica*

17 "Hingashakt" is prepared from

a) Asafoetida b) Juniper

c) Curry Leaf d) Kokum

18 South Mediterranean region is the native place of

a) Tamarind b) Juniper

c) Chilli d) Thyme

19 Pod of Tamarind is composed of

a) 55% pulp, 34% seed, 11% shell and fibre

b) 55% pulp, 34% seed, 11% shell

c) 45% pulp, 24% seed, 30% shell and fibre

d) 45% pulp, 24% seed, 30% shell

20 Juni-perin is obtained from

a) All Spice b) Juniper

c) Thyme d) Kokum

21 Composition of Juni-perin is

a) Mixture of tannins and sugar b) Mixture of phytin and sugar

c) Both a and b d) None of these

22 Saffron belongs to family

a) Cupressaceae b) Iridaceae

c) Lamaceae d) Clusiaceae

23 1kg of Saffron can be obtained from

a) 100 flowers b) 10000 flowers

c) 1.5 million flowers d) None of these

24 Madagasy Republic is the leading producer of

a) Kokum b) Fennel

c) Saffron d) Vanilla

25 Konkan Amrit is a variety of

a) Saffron b) Clove

c) Kokum d) Nutmeg

26 Curry Leaf is rich in

a) Calcium b) Potassium

c) Phosphorous d) Magnesium

27 Which of the following is a double seeded berry

a) Kokum b) All spice

c) Vanilla d) Tamarind

28 Seed rate of Fennel is

a) 5-6 kg/ha b) 6-10 kg/ha

c) 10-12 kg/ha d) 12-15 kg/ha

29 All Spice contains flavour of

a) Cinnamon, Vanilla and Kokum

b) Cardamom, Curry Leaf and Thyme

c) Cinnamon, Clove and Nutmeg

d) Fennel, Cumin and Chilli

30 "Ksenigin" is obtained from which part of Curry Leaf

a) Leaves b) Flowers

c) Seeds d) Roots

31 Seed rate of Cumin is

a) 20-25 kg/ha b) 15-20 kg/ha

c) 10-15 kg/ha d) 12-15 kg/ha

32 Pant Harithna is a variety of

a) Fenugreek b) Coriander

c) Cumin d) None of these

33 Seeds of Fenugreek contain

a) Diosgenin b) Linalool

c) Limone d) Phenol

34 "Muragin" is obtained from which part of Curry Leaf

a) Leaves b) Flowers

c) Seeds d) Roots

35 Which is the oldest known spice

a) Fenugreek b) Coriander

c) Tamarind d) Cinnamon

36 Clove belongs to which family

a) Myristicaceae b) Mytraceae

c) Fabaceae d) None of these

37 Cinnamon is commercially propagated by

a) Seeds b) Bark

c) Roots d) Rhizome

38 Srobha is a variety of

a) Clove b) Cinnamon

c) Turmeric d) Nutmeg

39 Which is the leading producer of Ginger in India

a) Punjab b) Chennai

c) Tamil Nadu d) Kerela

40 Ginger is native of

a) India b) Sri Lanka

c) South East Asia d) Indo-Burma

41 Golsey is a variety of

a) Large Cardamom b) Small Cardamom

c) Ginger d) Clove

42 Vazukha type of Small Cardamom is a cross between

a) PV-2 and Mudigree-1 b) Mysore and Malabar

c) Malabar and PV-2 d) Malabar and Mysore

43 Inflorescence type of Small Cardamom is

a) Raceme b) Panicle

c) Cyme d) None of these

44 Small Cardamom is propagated by

a) Roots b) Seeds

c) Cuttings d) Rhizome

45 Fruiting branches of Black Pepper are known as

a) Plagiotropes b) Geotropes

c) Orthotropes d) None of these

46 Largest producer of Black pepper is

a) USA b) Russia

c) Turkey d) Vietnam

47 Which country is known as "home of spices"

a) China b) USA

c) Brazil d) India

48 Top shootsof Black Pepper are known as

a) Plagiotropes b) Geotropes

c) Orthotropes d) None of these

49 What is the chromosome number of Cumin

a) 62 b) 48

c) 44 d) 14

50 Hanging shootsof Black Pepper are known as

a) Plagiotropes b) Geotropes

c) Orthotropes d) None of these

51 Iran is the native place of

a) Curry Leaf b) Saffron

c) Asafoetida d) Fennel

52 Which of the following is a perennial spice crop

a) Pepper b) Dill

c) Fennel d) Fenugreek

53 Which of the following is an annual spice crop

a) Cumin b) Turmeric

c) Both a and b d) Vanilla

54 Eurasia is the origin of

a) Nutmeg b) Sweet Flag

c) Dill d) Clove

55 Cineol is present in

a) Small Cardamom b) Ginger

c) Black Pepper d) None of these

56 Essential oil content of Asafoetida is

a) 5-6% b) 10-17%

c) 15-20% d) 21-25%

57 *Garcinia indica* is the botanical name of

a) Aniseed b) Bishop's Weed

c) Sweet Flag d) None of these

58 Economic part of clove is

a) Bark b) Unopened flower bud

c) Aril d) Fruit

59 Terbein is present in

a) Cinnamon b) Nutmeg

c) Clove d) Curry Leaf

60 Essential oil content of Cumin is

a) 2.5-3.5% b) 2.0-2.5%

c) 1.5-2.0% d) 1.0-1.5%

61 Botanical name of Sweet Flag is

a) *Acorus calamus* b) *Pimenta dioca*

c) *Pimpinella anisum* d) *Anethum graveolens*

62 Linalool is present in

a) Dill b) Sweet Flag

c) Kokum d) Coriander

63 Which of the following is not a variety of Cinnamon

a) Navashree b) Konkan Tej

c) Amulya d) Yercaud-1

64 Dried aril around the seed of nutmeg is called

a) Drupe b) Berry

c) Mace d) None of these

65 Average height of Nutmeg tree is

a) 8-10 meters b) 4-10 meters

c) 2-8 meters d) 2-6 meters

66 Pericarp of Nutmeg is a rich source of

a) Tannin b) Pectin

c) Fat d) None of these

67 Which of the following is a small seeded variety of Coriander

a) Sindhu b) Swathi

c) Merrocan d) Karan

68 Average yield of Cumin is

a) 2-5 q/ha b) 5-10 q/ha

c) 7-8 q/ha d) None of these

69 Jamaica is the major producer of

a) All Spice b) Nutmeg

c) Kokum d) Fennel

70 Hydroxy citric acid is present in

a) Kokum b) Vanilla

c) Chilli d) Tamarind

71 Curry Leaf belongs to family

a) Apiaceae b) Clusiaceae

c) Orchidaceae d) Rutaceae

72 Planting season of Saffron is

a) January- March b) April-June

c) July-September d) November-December

73 Major biting taste of Black Pepper is due to

a) Eugenol b) Piperine

c) Flavanoids d) Phenols

74 Curing of Cardamom is done by

a) Drying at hot temperature b) Drying at low temperature

c) Drying at medium temperature d) None of these

75 The term Allepy is related to which crop

a) Ginger b) Garlic

c) Nutmeg d) Turmeric

76 Trymyristicin is a major constituent of

a) Clove b) Nutmeg

c) All Spice d) Cinnamon

77 Vanillin is developed due to the action of

a) β-glycoside b) Amylase

c) Lipase d) None of these

78 Coumarin is the cheap substitute for

a) Kokum b) Curry Leaf

c) Cumin d) Vanilla

79 Which is the third largest seed spice after Coriander and Cumin

a) Clove b) Dill

c) Fenugreek d) None of these

80 Average weight of individual Nutmeg is

a) 10 g b) 30 g

c) 60 g d) 90 g

81 Which of the following is both a tropical and temperate crop

a) Nutmeg b) Clove

c) Cinnamon d) Fenugreek

82 Volatile oil of Nutmeg has

a) Pesticidal property b) Bactericidal property

c) Weedicidal property d) Both a and c

83 Which of the following is a seophyte

a) Fennel b) Large Cardamom

c) Small Cardamom d) Ginger

84 The mean annual rainfall for cardamom is

a) 1000-2000 mm b) 1500-5750 mm

c) 2000-4000 mm d) None of these

85 Average yield of Black Pepper is

a) 173 kg/ha b) 153 kg/ha

c) 273 kg/ha d) 253 kg/ha

86 Which country is the major importer and consumer of oleoresin (50%)

a) India b) China

c) Russia d) USA

87 Which state in India has the largest area under spices

a) Rajasthan b) Goa

c) Assam d) Punjab

88 Chromosome number of Curry leaf is

a) 12 b) 14

c) 18 d) 22

89 Acorin is present in

a) Dill b) Sweet Flag

c) Aniseed d) Kokum

90 Self-sterile variety of Black pepper is

a) Balankotta b) Kalluvali

c) Both a and b d) None of these

91 Sikkim is the largest producer of

a) Fennel b) Fenugreek

c) Large Cardamom d) Turmeric

92 Best sowing time for Cumin is

a) February b) April

c) July d) November

93 Harvesting season of Saffron is

a) March-April b) June-July

c) August-September d) October-November

94 Origin of Juniper is

a) Iran b) Africa

c) Netherlands d) Brazil

95 Which of the following is not a variety of fennel

a) RF-101 b) RF-125

c) RZ-209 d) RF-35

96 Alternate bearing habit is present in

a) Clove b) Fennel

c) Tamarind d) Both a and b

97 Seed rate of fenugreek is

a) 10 kg/ha b) 20 kg/ha

c) 25 kg/ha d) 35 kg/ha

98 *Trigonella foenum-graecum* is the scientific name of

a) Clove b) Fennel

c) Fenugreek d) Dill

99 Economic part of Vanilla is

a) Seed b) Leaves

c) Rhizome d) Fruit

100 Rio De Janerio is a variety of

a) Clove
b) Cardamom
c) Ginger
d) Nutmeg

101 Leading seed spice crop grown in India is

a) Clove
b) Cumin
c) Fennel
d) Coriander

102 Which of the following is incorrect

a) Clove- *Syzygium aromaticum*
b) Nutmeg- *Myristica fragrans*
c) Coriander- *Cuminum cyminum*
d) Small Cardamom- *Elettaria cardamomum*

103 Cumin belongs to family

a) Apiaceae
b) Rutaceae
c) Fabaceae
d) Lauraceae

104 Which of the following is correct

a) Black pepper- Lauraceae
b) Dill- Apiaceae
c) Fennel- Rutaceae
d) Kokum- Iridaceae

105 Guttiferae is the family of

a) Sweet Flag
b) Aniseed
c) All Spice
d) Kokum

106 Carvone is present in

a) Curry Leaf
b) Bishop's Weed
c) Dill
d) None of these

107 Poornima is a variety of

a) Black Pepper
b) Clove
c) Small Cardamom
d) Large Cardamom

108 Shoot cutting is used for the propagation of

a) Ginger
b) Turmeric
c) Fenugreek
d) Black Pepper

109 Which of the following is a mutant variety of Ginger

a) Himgiri
b) Surbhi
c) Suruchi
d) Varada

110 Which country is the major importer of Indian Pepper

a) Africa b) Indonesia

c) North America d) Brazil

111 Juniper belongs to family

a) Lamaceae b) Iridaceae

c) Clusiaceae d) Cupressaceae

112 Origin of Curry Leaf is

a) India b) Brazil

c) Canada d) USA

113 *Murraya koenigii* is the scientific name of

a) All Spice b) Dill

c) Curry Leaf d) Kokum

114 Which state is the leading producer of Coriander

a) Gujrat b) Tamil Nadu

c) Rajasthan d) Maharashtra

115 Which country is the major exporter of Cumin

a) Iran b) Iraq

c) Egypt d) Turkey

116 Botanical name of Cinnamon is

a) *Cinnamomum aromaticum* b) *Cinnamomum cyminum*

c) *Cinnamomum verum* d) None of these

117 Tree of Clove is

a) Medium sized and evergreen b) Medium sized and deciduous

c) Tall and evergreen d) Tall and deciduous

118 Average seed weight of Nutmeg is

a) 1-3 g b) 2-5 g

c) 6-7 g d) 8-9 g

119 Major producer of Clove is

a) USA b) China

c) India d) Indonesia

120 Nutmeg is

a) Monoecious b) Dioecious

c) Hermaphrodite d) None of these

121 Pratibha is a variety of

a) Clove b) Nutmeg

c) Cinnamon d) Turmeric

122 GC-1 is a variety of

a) Ginger b) Clove

c) Cumin d) Cinnamon

123 Kokum is

a) Monoecious b) Dioecious

c) Hermaphrodite d) None of these

124 Vanillin is extracted by

a) Solvent extraction b) Hydro alcoholic extraction

c) Super critical fluid extraction d) Hot fat extraction

125 Berries of All Spice are rich in

a) Vitamin A b) Vitamin D

c) Vitamin E d) Vitamin K

126 Curry Leaf is propagated by

a) Cuttings b) Rhizome

c) Suckers d) Seeds

127 The aromatic volatile components of spices are called

a) Spice Oil b) Spice Fat

c) Spice Gel d) Spice Paste

128 Which is known as Indian cassia

a) *C. cassia* b) *C. burmanni*

c) *C. lourerii* d) *C. tamala*

129 National Research Center for Seed Spices (ICAR) is located at

a) Ajmer b) Assam

c) Calicut d) Mysore

130 Cardamom Research Center is located at

a) Kerela
b) Tamil Nadu
c) Karnataka
d) Goa

131 Anthracnose of Pepper is caused by

a) *Colletotrichum gloeosporioides*
b) *Rhizoctonia solani*
c) *Sclerotium rolfsii*
d) None of these

132 Scientific name of Cardamom thrips is

a) *Conogethes punctiferalis*
b) *Sciothrips cardamom*
c) *Basilepta fulvicorne*
d) None of these

133 Soft rot or rhizome rot of Ginger is caused by

a) *Pythium aphanidermatum*
b) *P. vexans*
c) *P. myriotylum*
d) All of these

134 Leaf blotch of turmeric is caused by

a) *Taphrina maculans*
b) *Colletotrichum capsici*
c) *Pythium graminicolum*
d) None of these

135 Grenada is the second largest exporter of

a) Nutmeg
b) Clove
c) Cinnamon
d) Thyme

136 The fruits of Nutmeg are ready for harvest in about_______ months after flowering

a) 7 months
b) 8 months
c) 9 months
d) 10 months

137 Seeds of Fenugreek are_______ long and_______ broad respectively

a) 2.5-5 mm long and 2-5 mm broad
b) 3-4 mm long and 1-1.5 mm broad
c) 4.5-5.5 mm long and 1.5-2.5 mm broad
d) None of these

138 Powdery mildew of Fenugreek is caused by

a) *Ramularia foeniculi*
b) *Peronospora trigonellae*
c) *Erysiphe polygonii*
d) None of these

139 Cumin seeds germinate in

a) 5-6 days
b) 8-10 days
c) 10-14 days
d) None of these

140 Recommended dose of FYM for Cumin is

a) 8-10 t/ha
b) 15-20 t/ha
c) 20-25 t/ha
d) 25-30 t/ha

141 The first dose of nitrogen should be applied after how many days in Cumin

a) 20 DAS
b) 30 DAS
c) 40 DAS
d) 50 DAS

142 The earliest reference to use of dill seed in medicine goes back to

a) 700 BC
b) 600 BC
c) 500 BC
d) 400 BC

143 Two types of Dill that exist for cultivation are

a) European Dill and Indian Dill
b) Indian Dill and American Dill
c) African Dill and European Dill
d) None of these

144 Optimum temperature for flowering in Saffron is

a) 20-25°C
b) 15-20°C
c) 10-15°C
d) None of these

145 The finest quality Saffron is obtained from

a) Mongra Saffron
b) Lachha Saffron
c) Shahi Saffron
d) All of these

146 The ideal relative humidity for cultivation of Vanilla is

a) 60%
b) 70%
c) 80%
d) 90%

147 Cumin seeds are soaked for ________ hours before germination

a) 24
b) 48
c) 36
d) None of these

148 1st weeding and hoeing in fennel is done after how many days of sowing

a) 15 days
b) 25 days
c) 30 days
d) 40 days

149 Recommended dose of N:P:K for Coriander is

a) 20:30:20 kg/ha
b) 20:20:20 kg/ha
c) 30:20:30 kg/ha
d) None of these

150 Coriander can be grown successfully in soil with a pH of

a) 4-5
b) 6-7
c) 7-8
d) 8-9

Answer Key

1	d	2	c	3	b	4	b	5	a	6	c	7	a
8	b	9	c	10	d	11	c	12	b	13	c	14	c
15	d	16	b	17	a	18	d	19	a	20	b	21	a
22	b	23	c	24	d	25	c	26	a	27	b	28	c
29	c	30	a	31	d	32	b	33	a	34	b	35	d
36	b	37	a	38	c	39	d	40	c	41	a	42	b
43	b	44	d	45	a	46	d	47	d	48	c	49	d
50	b	51	c	52	a	53	c	54	c	55	a	56	b
57	d	58	b	59	b	60	a	61	a	62	d	63	c
64	c	65	b	66	b	67	d	68	c	69	a	70	a
71	d	72	c	73	b	74	b	75	d	76	b	77	a
78	d	79	c	80	c	81	d	82	c	83	b	84	b
85	c	86	d	87	a	88	c	89	b	90	c	91	c
92	d	93	d	94	c	95	c	96	a	97	c	98	c
99	d	100	c	101	d	102	c	103	a	104	b	105	d
106	c	107	a	108	d	109	b	110	c	111	d	112	a
113	c	114	c	115	a	116	c	117	a	118	c	119	d
120	b	121	d	122	c	123	b	124	b	125	a	126	d
127	a	128	d	129	a	130	c	131	a	132	b	133	d
134	a	135	a	136	c	137	a	138	c	139	c	140	b
141	c	142	a	143	a	144	b	145	c	146	c	147	b
148	c	149	a	150	b								

Sample Paper-1

1 *Canavalia ensiformis* is botanical name of

a) Sword Bean b) Winged bean

c) Jack Bean d) Cluster Bean

2 French Bean is

a) Day neutral b) Long Day

c) Short day d) None of these

3 Curry Leaf belongs to

a) Umbelliferae b) Moringaceae

c) Rutaceae d) Polygonaceae

4 Based on respiration rate, Tomato is classified as

a) Low b) Very High

c) Moderate d) Extremely high

5 Flower Head is edible part of which vegetable

a) Cauliflower b) Brocolli

c) Globe Artichoke d) Both B&C

6 International Potato Centre was established in

a) 1978 b) 1971

c) 1976 d) 1972

7 Palam Hriday is a colour rich variety of

a) Tomato b) Beet Root

c) Radish d) Carrot

8 Ca Oxalates , a toxic substance is found in which vegetable

a) Globe Artichoke b) EFY

c) Taro d) All of the above

9 Which of the following is PCR based marker

a) SSR b) RFLP

c) RAPD d) Both A&C

10 K, Ca elements are involved in

a) Energy storage and bonding
b) Regulators and carriers
c) Catalyzers and activators
d) Both A&B

11 "India Organic" is a

a) Trademark
b) Brand name
c) Certification Agency
d) Company

12 Gold Flakes" in Tomato is caused due to

a) K Toxicity
b) K Deficiency
c) Excess Ca –oxalates
d) Ca deficiency

13 In Indeterminate Tomatoes, inflorescence occurs at

a) At every node
b) At every 2nd node
c) At every 3rd node
d) At every 4th node

14 Which of the following is hardiest crop

a) Knol-khol
b) Kale
c) Cauliflower
d) Cabbage

15 In cucurbits, high temperature induces

a) Femaleness
b) Parthenocarpy
c) Maleness
d) No flowering

16 Male sterility found in Carrot is

a) CMS
b) GMS
c) CGMS
d) Both A&C

17 Akashin , a physiological disorder occurs due to

a) Boron deficiency
b) High Day temperature
c) High Night temperature
d) All of these

18 "Speckled Yellow" is a disorder of

a) Radish
b) Beet
c) Turnip
d) Both A&B

19 Inflorescence of sweet potato is

a) Racemose
b) Raceme
c) Catkin
d) Cymose

20 Vascular Streaking is present in

a) Beet
b) Sweet potato
c) EFY
d) Cassava

21 Which of the following is a dioecious vegetable

a) Kakrol
b) Pointed gourd
c) Ivy gourd
d) All of these

22 Seed rate of Sprouting Broccoli is

a) 100-200 g
b) 200-300 g
c) 300-400 g
d) 400-500 g

23 Jewel is a transgenic cultivar of

a) Sweet potato
b) Potato
c) Tomato
d) Summer squash

24 Tag colour of certified seed is

a) White
b) Blue
c) Opal green
d) Purple

25 Leaf silvering is a physiological disorder of

a) Summer squash
b) Pumpkin
c) Cucumber
d) Spine gourd

26 Arka Harit is a variety of

a) Palak
b) Pea
c) Bitter gourd
d) Bottle gourd

27 No. of petals in flower of cruciferae family are

a) 5
b) 6
c) 4
d) 8

28 Ancestor of cucumber is

a) *Cucumis colocynthis*
b) *C. anguria*
c) *C. hardwickii*
d) *C. hystrix*

29 Which vegetable is also known as "New World Crop"

a) Tomato
b) Chekurmanis
c) Cowpea
d) Tapioca

30 Edible part of Chicory is

a) Bud b) Leaves

c) Root d) Stem

31 Gajendra is a variety of

a) Tapioca b) EFY

c) Taro d) Yam

32 Sree Sahya is a variety of

a) EFY b) Taro

c) Cassava d) Yam

33 Base temperature of Lettuce is

a) 2°C b) 4.4°C

c) 5.5°C d) 13°C

34 Fuyu is a processed product of

a) Cassava b) Taro

b) EFY d) Yam

35 Which type of fruit is present in Okra

a) Pod b) Capsule

c) Siliqua d) Berry

36 Globe artichoke is a

a) C_3 Plant b) C_4 Plant

c) CAM d) None of these

37 Pusa Alankar belongs to

a) Summer squash b) Winter squash

c) Pumpkin d) Bottle gourd

38 Variety of Bottle gourd without crook neck

a) Pusa summer prolific long b) Arka Harit

c) Pusa Meghdhoot d) Arka Bahar

39 Red Colour in Chilli is due to

a) Lycopene b) Capsaicin

c) Xanthophyll d) Capxanthin

40 In Onion, temeprature is more important than day length in

a) Seed production b) Bulb Production

c) Both A&B d) None of these

41 Inflorescence type of pea and beans is

a) Cymose b) Racemose

c) Umbel d) Raceme

42 Isolation distance in Foundation seed in Pea is

a) 10m b) 20m

c) 5 m d) 40M

43 Arkel variety of pea is suitable for

a) Fresh market b) Dehydration

c) Both A&B d) None of these

44 Tapioca is propagated by

a) Seed b) Stakes

c) Tuber d) Corms

45 Sweet yam is another name of

a) Greater yam b) Lesser yam

c) White yam d) Water yam

46 Which vegetable is also known as "Queen of Kitchen"

a) Tomato b) Potato

c) Onion d) Garlic

47 In onion, "Neck fall" is the maturity index for

a) Rabi crop b) Kharief crop

c) Zaid crop d) All of these

48 Dehydration ratio in onion for Indian varieties is

a) 5:1 b) 6:1

c) 8:1 d) 10:1

49 Chromosome no. of Chinese cabbage is

a) 18 b) 20

c) 36 d) 24

50 Which of the following is Leaf curl resistant variety in Tomato

a) Arka Vardan
b) Arka Abha
c) Hissar Gaurav
d) Pusa Sheetal

51 Spinach and collard are..

a) Pothrebs or green.
b) Potherbs or salad.
c) Green or salad.
d) All of the above.

52 Which is a salad crop?

a) Lettuce.
b) Celery.
c) Both a and b.
d) Radish.

53 Cabbage contain a compound similar to

a) Phenylthiocarbamide.
b) Phenolthiocarbamide.
c) Phenylthiocarbamine
d) Phenolthiocarbamine

54 Leek is a

a) Legume
b) Leafy vegetable.
c) Bulb crop.
d) Root crop.

55 Scientific name of sweet corn is..?

a) *Zea mays convar. saccharata var. esculenta*
b) *Zea mays convar. saccharata var. rugosa*
c) *Zea mays convar. saccharata var. sativa*
d) None of the above.

56 Seed rate of onion is

a) 2-3kg/ha
b) 5-7 kg/ha
c) 7-10 kg/ha
d) 15-18 kg/ha

57 Tree onion is..?

a) Allium × viviparum
b) Allium × proliferum
c) Allium × prolifera
d) Allium × wakegi.

58 Which of the following is wind pollinated crop

a) Spinach
b) Okra
c) Beans
d) Beet root

59 Which of the following gourd is Diocious

a) Snake gourd
b) Pointed gourd
c) Cucumber
d) Squash

60 Blossom end rot in tomato is caused by

a) N deficiency b) B deficiency

c) K toxicity d) Mn deficiency

61 Bulbs (onion) are transformation of

a) Root b) Short stem

c) Long stem d) Tape root.

62 ________ Is an antioxidant rich variety of potato

a) Kufri Neelkanth. b) Kufri Prabha.

c) Kifri Abha. d) Kufri Kiran.

63 For ideal sugar accumulation in cucurbits suitable condition is

a) Warm nights and warm days b) Cool nights and warm days

c) Long days and warm nights d) Cool days and cool nights

64 Which one has spiny surface?

a) Pointed gourd. b) Sweet potato.

c) Chayote d) None of the above.

65 Golden acre is an ideal variety of cabbage for..?

a) Hills b) Plateau region

c) Both A and B d) Plains.

66 Main consideration for the cultivation of cabbage In india

a) Seed rate b) Club root disease.

c) Soil preparation d) Irrigation.

67 Seed rate required for cauliflower is..?

a) Lower than the seed rate of cabbage

b) More than the seed rate of cabbage

c) Equal to the seed rate of cabbage

d) Anything

68 Snow ball is the variety of cauliflower, ideal for _______ regions

a) Hills and plateau b) Hills and plains

c) Plains d) Hills

69 Which antioxidant compound is dominant in Brocoli

a) Anthocyanin b) Cryptoxanthins

c) Sulphoraphine d) Glucoraphane

70 The early varieties of cauliflower seedling are transplanted from raised-bed to field?

a) 15 days old seedlings
b) 20 days old seedlings
c) 25 days old seedlings
d) 30 days old seedlings.

71 The curd initiation stage in cauliflower after transplanting is..?

a) 15 days
b) 25 days.
c) 35 days
d) 40 days.

72 Gap filling is common in..?

a) Cauliflower
b) Cabbage.
c) Brinjal
d) All of the above

73 Whip tail is pronounced in..?

a) Acidic soil
b) Saline soil
c) Neutral soil
d) Acidic-Saline soil

74 Which is a induced mutant variety of Brinjal

a) KKM
b) MDU-1
c) PKM
d) PLR.

75 Spacing for hybrid brinjal is

a) 60 cm x 90 cm
b) 90 cm x75 cm
c) 60 cm x 60 cm
d) 90 cm x 60 cm

76 The established seedlings of brinjal need

a) Weekly irrigation
b) Fortnightly.
c) Monthly irrigation
d) At every 20 days.

77 The paired row system is adopted in brinjal

a) If flood irrigation is adopted
b) If canal irrigation is adopted
c) If drip irrigation is installed
d) All of the above.

78 Ideal temperature for effective pollination in tomato is

a) 18°C
b) 15°C
c) 21°C
d) 27°C

79 Earthing up is needed in

a) Potato
b) Brinjal
c) Sweet potato
d) All of the above

80 Scientific name of Knolkhol

a) Brassica oleracea var. botrytis

b) Brassica oleracea var. capitata

c) Brassica oleracea var. acephala

d) Brassica oleracea var. gongyloides

81 Recommended growth regulator for Brinjal

a) Triacontanol plus Sodium Borate b) GA3

c) Both A&B d) IAA

82 Clipping of the terminal portion of brinjal is done against

a) White fly b) Ash weevil

c) Shoot borer d) Aphid.

83 A variety of tomato suitable for rainfed conditions

a) Paiyur b) IIHR 709.

c) CO1 d) Kalyanpur selection.

84 Select the induced mutant variety of tomato

a) CO3 b) PKM 1.

c) Both A and B d) CO2

85 Azospirillum and Phosphobacteria are applied in tomato field

a) Before field preparation b) During field preparation

c) After sowing d) Before flowering.

86 Varieties of tomato are preferred for poly-house

a) Determinate b) Indeterminate.

c) Semi-determinate d) All of the above.

87 Quonset type, curved roof type and gable roof type green houses are classified as per

a) Glazing b) Number of span

c) Structure d) Environmental control.

88 The characteristics feature of Arka sujat (Ridge gourd) is

a) High yield

b) Resistant to red pumpkin beetle

c) The first male is produced on 13th node

d) The first female is produced on 13thnode

89 Stalking is practiced in

a) Tomato
b) Cowpea.
c) Pointed gourd
d) All of the above.

90 Maximum acidity in tomato is found in which stage.

a) Pink stage
b) Green stage
c) Mature stage
d) Turning stage

91 Which of the following varieties of chilli is multiple disease resistant

a) NP-46A
b) Punjab Surukh
c) Bhaskar
d) Puri Red

92 Vegetable of 20th century is

a) Broad bean
b) Winged bean
c) French bean
d) Pea

93 Directorate on onion and Garlic is located at

a) Rajagurunagar
b) Nasik
c) Pune
d) Anand

94 In onion critical crop weed competition occurs at

a) 20-30 DAP
b) 30-60 DAP
c) 60-80 DAP
d) 70-90 DAP

95 Optimum storage conditions for onion

a) 4%RH, 5 0C Temp.
b) 65-75%RH, 0 0C Temp.
C) 75-95%RH, 100C Temp.
d) 10-20%, 7 0C Temp.

96 Variety developed through selfing and massing in onion

a) Agrifound Red
b) Brown spanish
c) Cream gold
d) Pusa madhir

97 Dominant sugar in carrot is

a) Glucose
b) Sucrose
c) Both A and B
d) Fructose

98 Carrot splitting occurs due to

a) Ca deficiency
b) Boron deficiency
c) N deficiency
d) Both B and C

99 Optimum temperature fo bulb formation in onion

a) 20-30°C b) 25-35°C

c) 15-25°C d) 15-18°C

100 Seed rate of Broad bean

a) 70-100 kg/ha b) 40-50 kg/ha

c) 120-150 kg/ha d) 90-110 kg/ha

Sample Paper-2

1 As per the RDA (Recommended Dietary Allowances), an adult man should consume

a) 200g green leafy vegetable, 100 g tubers, 100 other vegetables

b) 200 g tubers, 100 g legumes, 100 g leafy vegetables

c) 200 g roots and tubers, 100 g green leafy vegetable and 100 g other vegetables

d) None

2 The change in chromosome number which involves entire set of genome is called

a) Aneuploidy b) Euploidy

c) Trisomy d) Monosomy

3 Post harvest application of growth regulators has been found to

a) Decrease shelf life of vegetables

b) Extend shelf life of vegetables

c) Has no effect on the shelf life of vegetable

d) None of the above

4 Central vegetable breeding station was shifted from Katrain to IARI New Delhi in year

a) 1955 b) 1949

c) 1954 d) 1948

5 For a longer shelf life, the tomato fruits should have

a) Low polygalacturonase activity

b) High polygalacturonase activity tables

c) Low lycopene

d) High lycopene

6 Most fraction of TSS is due to

a) Proteins, cellulose, pectic substances, etc.

b) Sugars, organic acids, lipids, minerals etc

c) Nucleic acids

d) None

7 Raphanobrassica was discovered by

a) Mendel b) Nagaheru

c) Karpechenko d) Blakeslee

8 The effect of cytokinins is more conspicuous especially in

a) Root vegetables b) Leafy vegetables

c) Bulb vegetables d) Same effect in all

9 For good plant growth C: N ratio in soil must be

a) Narrow b) Broad

c) Both d) None

10 Seed rate per ha for cabbage is approximately

a) 5-6 kg b) 600-750 g

c) 3-4 kg d) None

11 Chicory and Endive, both belong to family

a) Araceae b) Apiaceae

c) Asteraceae d) None

12 Which of the following is not a self pollinated crop?

a) Lettuce b) Chicory

c) Potato d) None

13 Cucumbers are a fair source of

a) Vitamin C b) Carotenes

c) Both d) None

14 Sauer krat is prepared from

a) Knol khol b) Cauliflower

c) Kale d) Cabbage

15 Which of thefollowing is the most potent synthetic cytokinin?

a) GA3 b) N6-benzyl adenine (Ba)

c) N6-benzyl cysteine d) (2) & (3)

16 Additive genetic variance is

a) Heritable non- fixable b) Heritable fixable

c) Non-heritable non fixable d) Non-heritable fixable

17 Seed rate per ha for carrot is approximately

a) 10-12 kg
b) 600-700 g
c) 5-6 kg
d) 25-30 kg

18 Root crops are highly cross pollinated due to genetic mechanism of

a) Protogyny
b) Protandry
c) Self incompatibility
d) None

19 All cole crops have originated from

a) Brassica oleracea var *sylvestris*
b) B.oleracea var *gongylodes*
c) *B. oleracea* var *caulorapa*
d) None

20 The phenomenon of a single major gene affecting more than a character is known as

a) Penetarance
b) Pleiotropy
c) Variable expressivity
d) Linkage

21 Minimum purity % for foundation seed in cole crops is

a) 99%
b) 100%
c) 98%
d) 95%

22 To reduce the storage decay effectively, root crops should be given a pre storage dip treatment in"0.1% solution of

a) N6-benzyl adenine
b) Coconut water
c) Sodium o-phenyl phenate (SOPP)
d) None

23 The process of DNA synthesis from RNA is called

a) Transcription
b) Reverse transcription
c) Translation
a) Reverse translation

24 Minimum purity % for certified seed in cole crops

a) 95%
b) 98%
c) 96%
a) 95 %

25 Substitution of one purine by another purine is called

a) Addition
b) Transition
c) Deletion
d) Transversion

26 Primary gene pool refers to

a) GP1
b) GP2
c) GP3
d) All of the above

27 Which of the following plants resembles a sunflower plant?

a) Globe artichoke
b) Jersusalen Artichoke
c) Asparagus
d) Okra

28 Asparagus is a

a) Dioecious and a cool season crop
b) Dioecious and a warm season crop
c) Monoecious and a cool season crop
d) Monoecious and a warm season crop

29 A peptide bond is formed by

a) Aldehyde and carboxyl groups of two amino acids
b) Aldehyde and amino groups of two amino acids
c) Carboxyl and hydroxyl groups of two amino acids
d) Carboxy and amino groups of two amino acids

30 For the purpose of dehydration, the brinjal fruits must have

a) High dry matter and high phenolics content
b) High dry matter and low phenolics content
c) Low dry matter and high phenolics content
d) Low dry matter and low phenolics content

31 The male sterile line is referred as

a) A-Line
b) B-Line
c) R-Line
d) M-Line

32 To reduce the rate of ethylene production respiration and yellowing in broccoli, dipping at 0.01 M for 3 minutes at 20° C is recommended in which solution

a) Sodium 0°-phenyl phenate (SOPP)
b) CaCl2 solution
c) Sodium benzoate solution
d) None of the above

33 In sporophytic system of self incompatibility, full fertility will result from

a) S1 S2 x S1 S3
b) S1 S3 x S3 S4
c) S1 S2 X S2 S3
d) S2 S3 X S1 S2

34 Genes governing cytoplasmic inheritance are called

a) Plasma genes
b) Cytogenes
c) Cytoplasmic genes
d) All of the above

35 Clonal degeneration may occur by

a) Mutation b) Diseases

c) Both d) None

36 Post harvest application of which of the following markedly retards ripening of tomato

a) Auxins b) GA3

c) Cytokinins d) None

37 In green house frame works, iron is galvanized with

a) Aluminium to increase strength b) Zinc to prevent corrosion

c) Copper to increase life d) None of the above

38 Pusa sheetal is a variety of Tomato suitable for _________ regions

a) Low temperature b) Sub-temperature

c) High temperature d) All of the above

39 The basic chromosome number is denoted as

a) X b) 2x

c) N d) 2n

40 Gametophytic self incompatibility is prevalent in some plants of family

a) Solanaceae b) Brassicaceae

c) Both d) None

41 For certified seed production, the minimum isolation distance to be kept in cabbage

a) 100m b) 10m

c) 50m d) 1000m

42 Which pigment responsible for red colour in tomato

a) Anthocyanin b) Lycopene

c) Capsanthin d) None of the above

43 The process of bringing wild species under cultivation is known as

a) Domestication b) Acclimatization

c) Introduction d) All of the above

44 The development of lycopene is highest at which temperature

a) >40°c b) 25-30°C

c) 21-24°C d) None of the above

45 Movement of plant pests in response to light is known as

a) Photoperiodium
b) Photomovement
c) Phototropism
d) Photogenism

46 Which of the following conditions favour cross pollination

a) Dioecy
b) Heterogamy
c) Both
d) None

47 Meloidogyne species is

a) Sedentary endoparasite
b) Migratory endoparasite
c) Semi endoparasite
d) Ectoparasite

48 The parent which denotes desirable gene in backcross programme is called as

a) Donor parent
b) Non-recurrent parent
c) Both
d) None

49 For taking early crop in tomato which type of soil is preferred?

a) Sandy loam
b) Clay loam
c) Silty foam
d) All of the above

50 Laws of Mendel govern the inheritance of

a) Oligogenic traits
b) Polygenic traits
c) Both
d) None

51 Senescence that causes yellowing can effectively be retarded by pre- or post harvest applications of 2 (at 5-15 ppm)

a) IBA
b) NAA
c) BA(N6-benzyl adenine)
d) None

52 Pruning and training is generally followed in _________ tomatoes

a) Determinate
b) In determinate
c) Both A and B
d) None of the above

53 Reciprocal recurrent selection is used to improve

a) Gca
b) Sca
c) Both
e) None

54 Post harvest application of which of the following metabolic inhibitors is effective in controllingsprouting of tuber and bulb crops

a) Malic hydrazide (MH)
b) Chloro-isopropyl-carbonate (CIPC)

c) Methyl ester of naphthalene acetic acid (MENA)

d) All of the above

55 Great Irish potato famine occurred due to infection by

a) *Alternaria solani* b) *Fusarium oxysporium*

c) *Xanthomonas campesrtis* d) *Phytophthora infestans*

56 Which of the following methods is used to extract seeds from tomato fruits?

a) Fermentation method b) Acid treatment

c) Alkali treatment d) All of the above

57 Cracking in tomato fruits is due to deficiency of

a) Calcium b) Boron

c) Zinc b) All of the above

58 A synthetic variety is a mixture of several

a) Hybrids b) Purelines

c) Inbreds with good sca d) Inbreds with good gca

59 Deficiency of calcium is soil may result in ___________ of fruits

a) Cracking b) Blossom end rot

c) Sun scald d) All of the above

60 Vitamin C deficiency in human causes

a) Hypoglacemia b) Scurvey

c) Marasmus d) All of the above

61 Heterobeltiosis is estimated over

a) Mid parent b) Inferiorparent

c) Popular variety d) Better parent

62 Inability of a hybrid to produce viable off springs is called

a) Hybrid breakdown b) Hybrid in viability

c) Hybrid sterility d) Male sterility

63 Which is a common feature in brinjal?

a) Herterostyly b) Self incompatability

c) Both A and B d) None of the above

64 Synthesis of solanine in potato is inhibited by

a) Alar (N,N dimethyl aminosuccinamic acid)

b) Malic hydrozide (MH)

c) None

d) Both

65 Fruit setting is maximum in which flower of brinjal ?

a) Short styled b) Medium styled

c) Long styled d) Pseudo short styled

66 Allogamy leads to

a) Homozygosity b) Prepotency

c) Heterozygosity d) Inbreeding

67 The term auxin was first used by fruits Went in

a) 1916 b) 1926

c) 1936 d) 1946

68 Which is an extra early bearing cultivar of brinjal?

a) Pusa purple cluster b) Pusa purple round

c) Pusa purple long d) None of the above

69 The term Heterosis was coined by

a) Shull (1941) b) Hull (1945)

c) East (1908) d) Davenport (1908)

70 The processing varieties of potato to be used for chip making should have

a) High tuber dry matter content b) Low reducing sugars

c) Both d) None

71 India enacted PPV and FR Act in year

a) 1978 b) 1991

c) 2001 d) Not yet

72 Auxin occurs in

a) Free state b) Bound state

c) Bolt face and bound state d) None of the above

73 Seed plot technique was developed in potato for production of

a) Dormant seed tubers
b) Virus free seed tubers
c) True potato seeds
d) None

74 Triticale was developed through intergeneric cross between

a) Sweet William and Carnation
b) Cotton and tobacco
c) Tobacco and Wheat
d) Bread Wheat and rye

75 Cassava belongs to family

a) Solanaceae
b) Euphorbiaceae
c) Chenopodisceae
d) Malvaceae

76 Vitamin C deficiency in humans results in

a) Marasmus
b) Scurvy
c) Night blindness
d) All of the above

77 Taro is commonly grown in

a) Temperate areas
b) Tropical areas
c) Frigid areas
d) None

78 Recalcitrant crop species are maintained in

a) Seed gene banks
b) Field gene banks
c) Both
d) None

79 White yam belongs to genus Dioscorea and species

a) *Rotundata*
b) *Elata*
c) *Esculenta*
d) None

80 Cross pollination is associated with

a) Cleistogamy
b) Chasmogamy
c) Dichogamy
d) All of the above

81 Gibberellins were first discovered by plant pathologist in Japan in

a) 1920s
b) 1930s
c) 1940s
d) 1950s

82 In Jerusalem Artichoke, which part of the plant is edible

a) Leaves
b) Twigs
c) Stem
d) Tubers

83 An ideal greenhouse covering material should

a) Transmit sufficient visible light b) Absorb some UV light

c) Have long life d) All of the above

84 Which certificate is issued when sampling of seeds is done according to ISTA rules by an approvedofficial body?

a) Blue seed lot certificate b) Green seed lot certificate

c) Orange seed lot certificate d) None

85 Sweet potato is a

a) Self-pollinated crop b) Cross-pollinated crop

c) Non-flowering crop d) None

86 The physiological effects of auxins include

a) Cell elongation

b) Secondary growth

c) Apical dominance and rooting of cuttings

d) All of the above

87 Gene for gene hypothesis was proposed by

a) Nelson (1973) b) Flor (1956)

c) Vander Plank (1963) d) Robenson (1971)

88 Elephant foot yam belongs to genus

a) Colocasia b) Dioscoea

c) Amorphophilus d) Ipomea

89 Separation of a field with a variety to a prescribed distance from that of another variety to avoidcontamination is called as

a) Quarantine b) Isolation

c) Rouging d) Field inspection

90 The pathway of auxin particularly IAA synthesis involves the amino acid

a) Tryptophase b) Lysine

c) Cysteine d) None

91 Tomato variety Pusa hybrid -1 is suitable for which regions

a) Low temperature b) High temperature

c) Sub-tropical d) All of the above

92 In yams tubers show dormancy of

a) About 3 years

b) About 3 months

c) About 3 weeks

d) Do not show dormancy

93 A nullisomic individual is represented by

a) 2n-1 b) 2n-2

c) 2n+1 d) 2n+2

94 The mechanisms for synthesis of auxins involves

a) Removal of the amino acid group and the terminal carboxyl group from the side chain of precursor amino acid

b) Removal of the amino acid group and the carboxyl group from the side chain of precursor amino acid

c) Addition removal

d) None

Sample Paper-3

1 The variation present within a pureline is -

a) Genetic and heritable

b) Environmental and non-heritable

c) Cytoplasmic and heritable

d) Cytoplasmic and heritable

2 Clonal degeneration may occur by -

a) Mutation b) Diseases

c) Both d) None

3 Which of the following is known as stress hormone -

a) ABA b) GA

c) Ethylene d) None

4 Stress in plants leads to accumulation of -

a) Carbohydrates b) Proline

c) Vitamin d) All of above

5 The foliar spray of PCPA 50-100 ppm at the flowering stage increases the fruit set in tomato at -

a) Low temperature b) High temperature

c) Both at low and high temperature d) None of the above

6 Minimum isolation distance in okra for production of certified seed is-

a) 200 m b) 50 m

c) 1000 m d) 10 m

7 D2 statistic helps in assessing -

a) Genetic divergence b) Genetic variability

c) Narrow sense heritability d) None

8 The characteristic bitter taste in bitter gourd is due to -

a) Luffein b) Momordicin

c) Solanum d) None of the above

9 Under incompatible reaction, lack of interaction between the products of genes for resistance and avirulence produces-

a) Resistance reaction b) Susceptible reaction

c) Immune reaction d) Tolerance

10 To enhance ripening of tomato fruits ethrel @ -

a) 1000 ppm is effective at the tirbe of initiation of ripening

b) 2000 ppm is effective at the time of initiation of ripening

c) 3000 ppm is effective at the time of initiation of ripening

d) 4000 ppm is effective at the time of initiation of ripening

11 When two species of same genes are crossed, it is known as -

a) Inter specific hybridization b) Intra generic hybridization

c) Both d) None

12 Homozygonity increase with continued -

a) Selfing b) Inbreeding

13 Multiline varieties are mixtures of several purelines with -

a) Similar agronomic traits and same gene for resistance

b) Different agronomic traits and same gene for resistance

c) Different agronomic traits and different genes for resistance

d) Similar agronomic traits and different genes for resistance

14 Which of the following seeds has poor longevity -

a) Chilli b) Cucurbits

c) Onion d) Kale

15 Which of the following cucurbit is vegetatively propagated -

a) Ash gourd b) Pointed gourd

c) Bitter gourd d) None of the above

16 Fixation of heterosis may be achieved by -

a) Vegetable propagation b) Apomixes

c) Balanced lethal system d) All of the above

17 The bulk method of breeding was first used by -

a) Mendel b) Shull

c) Kempthorne d) Nilsson-Ehle

18 The character to be transferred in Back-cross method must have -

a) High variability b) High heritability

c) High linkage d) None

19 Which of the following is known as stress hormone? -

a) ABA b) Proline

c) Auxin d) Ethylene

20 Application of 2,4,-D @ 2 ppm at flowering -

a) Induces parthenocarpy

b) Increases fruit set

c) Advances fruit maturity and increases total yield

d) All of the above

21 Which of the following is a single seeded cucurbit? -

a) Pointed gourd b) Chow-chow

c) As gourd d) None of the above

22 An inbred variety cross is also known as -

a) Poly cross b) Top cross

c) Single cross d) Three way cross

23 Fruit set in chill can be improved by application of -

a) GA3 @ 10-100 ppm b) NA @ 20-200 ppm

c) CCC @ 1000 ppm d) All of the above

24 In watermelon, the most important judging indication for maturity is -

a) Dull sound b) Metallic sound

c) Size of the fruit d) None of the above

25 All the selection schemes cause -

a) increase in total genetic variance

b) Decrease in total genetic variance

c) No effect on total genetic variance

d) None

26 A cross between an inbred and an open pollinated variety is known as-

a) Single cross b) Top cross

c) Three way cross d) Double cross

27 Amaranthus is a rich source of -

a) Vitamin D
b) Vitamin E
c) Proteins
d) None

28 Evaluation of inbreds may be done by -

a) Top cross test
b) Dialed method
c) LxT method
d) All of the above

29 According to Falconer, the magnitude of average heterosis in F1 is given as -

a) H=dy
b) H-D2y
c) H= dy2
d) H = d2y2

30 Vegetables are primarily composed of -

a) Carbohydrates
b) Water
c) Water
d) Fiber

31 In cauliflower, application of GA4+ GA7 @ 80 mg/litre of water -

a) Shortened period from transplanting to harvest
b) Increased period from transplanting to harvest
c) No effect was observed.
d) Depends on the temperature

32 Most common sex expression in cucurbits is -

a) Monoecism
b) Gynoecism
c) Dioecism
d) All of the above

33 Heterosis to a large extent, is due to -

a) Dominance gene action
b) Additive gene action
c) Both
d) None

34 Which growth regulator is useful for fruit set at high temperature in tomato? -

a) Auxin
b) Ethylene
c) Gibberellin
d) ABA

35 Poinsette is a most popular variety of -

a) Bottle gourd
b) Cucumber
c) Bitter gourd
d) None of the above

36 Inbreeding leads to -

a) Reduction in vigour b) Increase in homozygosity

c) Reduction in yield d) All of the above

37 Growth regulator which improve fruit set in tomato is -

a) 2-4-D b) GA

c) MH d) Ethephon

38 Little leaf disease of brinjal is caused by -

a) Virus b) Bacteria

c) Mycoplasma like organisms- d) Cytoplasmic and heritable

39 Thomas Fairchild produced first artificial hybrid by crossing sweet William and carnation, which was called as -

a) Fairchild's dolly b) Fairchild's hybrid

c) Fairchild's donkey d) Fairchild's mule

40 Which of the following is used to check sprouting of onion storage?

a) NAA b) GA

c) MH d) PCPA

41 Which is an indication for edible maturity in slicing cucumber? -

a) White spine colour b) Black spine colour

c) Brown spine colour d) None of the above

42 Progeny test was developed by -

a) Johanuser b) Louis Pasteur

c) Louis de vilmorint d) Charles Darwin

43 Dormancy in potato can be broken by use of -

a) Thiourea b) Ethylene chlorohydrin

c) Potassium thiocynate d) All of the above

44 White heart at central position is an indication of __________ in fruits of watermelon -

a) Poor quality b) Maturity

c) Good quality d) None of the above

45 Correlation coefficients are split into measures of direct and indirect effects of independent variables on dependent variable through -

a) Correlation analysis b) Covariance analysis

c) Path analysis d) None

46 Which of the following is used as androcide?

a) GA3 b) MH-0.4-0.5%

c) NAA d) None

47 Yellow tinge/ Brown spot on the fruit of watermelon where it touches the ground is an indication of -

a) Maturity b) Poor quality

c) Good quality d) None of the above

48 The hyper sensitive response is triggered by certain unique molecules called -

a) Elicitors b) Phenols

c) R-proteins d) None of the above

49 Which is not a cytokinin? -

a) BA b) Zeatin

c) Etheral d) Kinetin

50 Which is a seedless variety of watermelon? -

a) Arka manik b) Pusa bedana

c) Arka jyoti d) None of the above

51 In pedigree selection, individual plants are selected from

a) F1 b) F2

c) F1 and F1 d) F2 and subsequent generations

52 The law stating that characters found in one species also occur in other related species is known as -

a) Law of segregation

b) Law of homologous series in variation

c) Law of diversity

d) None

53 Sex expression in cucurbits is manipulated by -

a) AGNO3 b) GA3

c) Ethereal d) All of the above

54 In a Vr-Wr graph, when the regression line passes through the origin, it indicates -

a) No dominance b) Partial dominance

c) Complete dominance d) Over Dominance

55 Dry shell of __________ is used for making murical instruments -

a) Bitter gourd
b) Pumpkin
c) Bottle gourd
d) None of the above

56 The characters whose performance depends on a specific environment are known as -

a) Polygenic characters
b) Oligogenic characters
c) Threshold characters
d) None

57 Which of the following is responsible for controlling of fruit draps?

a) Auxin
b) Gibberlins
c) Cytokinins
d) Ethylene

58 Semi-pole varieties of French bean are ______plants.

a) Short day
b) Long day
c) Day neutral
d) None

59 Over dominance hypothesis was proposed by -

a) East, 1908
b) Shull, 1908
c) Both
d) None

60 In the condition of dichogamy, stamens and pistils -

a) Mature at same time
b) Mature at different times
c) Do not mature at all
d) None of the above

61 Growth regulator related with abscission of leaves is -

a) ABA
b) Ethylene
c) GA
d) Cytokinin

62 Chief objective of hybridisation is to -

a) Create variation
b) increase yield
c) Improve quality
d) None

63 The various sources of make sterile cytoplasm are -

a) Spontaneous mutation
b) Induced mutation
c) Inter specific hybridization
d) All of the above

64 Which growth regulator, is commonly used as weedicide -

a) ABA
b) IBA
c) NAA
d) 2,4 -D

65 Supplementary gene action produces a ration of -

a) 13:3
b) 9:6:1
c) 9:7
d) 9:3:4

66 Components of genetic variance are estimated through -

a) Diallel
b) Line x Tester
c) Generation means
d) All of the above

67 Cytokinins are -

a) Synthesized in roots and transported to shoots
b) Synthesized in shoots and transported to roots
c) Both
d) None

68 Polygenic traits are considerably affected by -

a) Environment
b) Major genes
c) Oligogenic traits
d) None

69 Protein denaturation occurs at -

a) Lethal temperatures
b) Near lethal temperatures
c) Both
d) None

70 Ability of a gene to express itself in all individuals that carry them is called -

a) Expressivity
b) Penetrance
c) Luxuriance
d) Pleiotropy

71 Self-in compatibility may be temporarily suppressed by -

a) Bud pollination
b) Increased CO
c) Double pollination
d) All of the above

72 A chemical or physical agent that induces mutation is called as -

a) Mutator
b) Mutant
c) Mutagen
d) Muton

73 Genetic diversity can be assessed through -

a) D2Statistic
b) Metroglyph analysis
c) Both
d) None

74 The gene interaction producing the ratio of 12:3:1 is called -

a) Inhibitory gene action
b) Duplicate gene action
c) Complementary gene action
d) Masking gene action

75 For higher female to male ratio in bottle gourd the plants are sprayed with boron at 2-4 leaf stage at concentration of -

a) 20 ppm
b) 3 ppm
c) 10 ppm
d) None

76 During melesis, the exchange of chromation material between homologous chromosomes occurs during -

a) Linkage
b) Segregation
c) Crossing over
d) None

77 Maturation of male and female reproductive organs of a hermaphrodite flower at different times is known as -

a) Dicliny
b) Dioecy
c) Dichogamy
d) Herkogamy

78 Contact and infection stages of disease development being greatly affected by environment,provide the means for -

a) Disease avoidance
b) Disease tolerance
c) Disease escape
d) Disease resistance

79 Cracking in tomato fruits is due to deficiency of -

a) Calcium
b) Boron
c) Zinc
d) All of the above

80 Hypersensitive reaction represents a case of -

a) Susceptible reaction
b) Resistance reaction
c) Both
d) None

81 Complete absence of symptoms of a disease even after hast is exposed to the pathogen is -

a) An immune reaction
b) Complete resistance
c) Disease escape
d) None

82 The inflorescence in turnip is, on the main stem -

a) Terminal raceme
b) Umbel
c) Cyme
d) None

83 The variation present within a pureline is -

a) Genetic and heritable

b) Environmental and non-heritable

c) Cytoplasmic and heritable

d) Cytoplasmic and heritable

84 Gene for gene relationship between host and pathogen was postulated by -

a) Biffer in 1905
b) Blakeslee in 1904
c) Flor in 1956
d) None

85 In protogyny, stigma becomes receptive -

a) Before dehiscence
b) After dehiscence
c) At dehiscence
d) None

86 ___________is a bacterial wilt resistant variety of tomato -

a) BRW-5
b) BT-10
c) LE-79_s.
d) None

87 Percentage of impurity in a seed sample is known as -

a) Real value of seed
b) Test weight
c) Seed viability
d) Dockage

88 The vertifolia effect leads to an epidemic development in a variety carrying mainly -

a) Vertical resistance genes
b) Horizontal resistance genes
c) Both
d) None

89 TSS estimated as -

a) Specific gravity
b) Refractive index
c) Both
d) None

90 Cryopreservation can be adopted for preservation of which type of seed-

a) Orthodox
b) Recalcitrant
c) Both A and B
d) None

91 Removal of immature anthers (or androecium) from hermaphiodite flower is known as -

a) Bud pollination
b) Anthesis
c) Emasculation
d) Dehiscence

92 The Seed Act was passed in India in -

a) 1966 b) 1969

c) 1968 d) None

93 Isolation of a plant to prevent spread of diseases is known as -

a) Isolation distance b) Escape

c) Time isolation d) Quarantine

94 The glucosinolates present in Brassica Spp. seeds are -

a) Carcinogenic b) Goitrogenic

c) Neurotoxic d) None

95 When whole layers of shoot tip meristems are affected by mutations, it results in -

a) Periclinal chimera b) Sectorial chimera

c) Mericlinal chimera d) All of the above

96 The two fundamental philosophies for regulating seed quality are -

a) European philosophy b) North American philosophy

c) Both A and B d) None

97 An endonuclease which cuts a DNA molecule within or near a site is known -

a) Molecular marker b) Restriction enzyme

c) Ligase d) None

98 Most of the mutations are -

a) Desirable and recessive b) Undesirable and recessive

c) Desirable and dominant d) Undesirable and dominant

99 During meiosis, an amphidiploids behaves as -

a) A haploid b) A Diploid

c) A Triploid d) None

100 Tetrazolium test is performed to find out _________ of seed .

a) Dormancy stage b) Viability

c) Vigour d) None